My Inspirational Favorites

My Inspirational Favorites

Norman Vincent Peale

A Giniger Book
published in association with

HarperSanFrancisco
A Division of HarperCollins*Publishers*

FIRST EDITION

Library of Congress Cataloging-in-Publication Data

My inspirational favorites / [edited by] Norman Vincent Peale.—1st ed.
      p. cm.
  ISBN 0–06–066453–3 (alk. paper)
  1. Literature—Collections. 2. Inspiration—Literary collections.
3. Conduct of life—Literary collections.   I. Peale, Norman Vincent.
PN6014.M9 1992
810.8´038—dc20   91–58989
                                                        CIP

92 93 94 95 96 ❖ HAD 10 9 8 7 6 5 4 3 2 1

This edition is printed on recycled, acid-free paper that meets the American National Standards Institute Z39.48 Standard.

Contents

A Word to the Reader

IN THIS BOOK, I am privileged to share some of the essays, poems, stories, and portions of books that have been inspirations to me in my lifetime of reading.

I have made my selections not as a literary critic but because I like them. They have inspired and helped me, and I hope they do the same for you. Many people have told me that these particular pieces have appealed to them also.

If I had collected all my favorites from my reading over the years, they would make up an enormous volume. Instead, I have chosen to assemble a little book that can be easily carried or read in bed. I have tried sincerely to make it a book that will be a joy to have in a personal library. May you find it a rewarding and pleasant companion for many a happy hour.

Norman Vincent Peale

NOT MANY PEOPLE TODAY have heard of Henry Drummond, but toward the end of the last century he was widely known throughout Great Britain and the United States. A Scottish geologist who taught natural science and later theology in a Glasgow college, Drummond had a burning passion to speak and write profound truths about Christianity in simple terms that could be easily understood.

In 1883 he wrote "The Greatest Thing in the World," a speech he gave in Africa and, in 1887, all over the United States. Reports on this speech attested to the thrill audiences felt when they heard Drummond talk about "the supreme good," Love. And when his speech was printed into a little book, it sold more than 350,000 copies—an astounding number for the day.

His passionate belief made him one of the most popular figures of his time. I hope you will enjoy and profit from reading this great scientific thinker of the preceding century.

It was Henry Drummond's custom, at the beginning of each lecture, to read from the Bible, I Corinthians, chapter 13, which follows:

THOUGH I SPEAK with the tongues of men and of angels, and have not Love, I am become as sounding brass, or a tinkling cymbal. And though I have the gift of prophecy, and understand all mysteries, and all knowledge; and though I have all faith, so that I could remove mountains, and have not Love, I am nothing. And though I bestow all my goods to feed the poor, and though I give my body to be burned, and have not Love, it profiteth me nothing.

1

Love suffereth long, and is kind;
Love envieth not;
Love vaunteth not itself, is not puffed up,
Doth not behave itself unseemly,
Seeketh not her own,
Is not easily provoked,
Thinketh no evil;
Rejoiceth not in iniquity, but rejoiceth in the truth;
Beareth all things, believeth all things, hopeth all
things, endureth all things.

Love never faileth: but whether there be prophecies, they shall fail; whether there be tongues, they shall cease; whether there be knowledge, it shall vanish away. For we know in part, and we prophesy in part. But when that which is perfect is come, then that which is in part shall be done away. When I was a child, I spake as a child, I understood as a child, I thought as a child: but when I became a man, I put away childish things. For now we see through a glass, darkly; but then face to face: now I know in part; but then shall I know even as also I am known. And now abideth faith, hope, Love, these three; but the greatest of these is Love.

The Greatest Thing in the World

Henry Drummond (1851–1897)

EVERY ONE has asked himself the great question of antiquity as of the modern world: What is the *summum bonum*—the supreme good? You have life before you. Once only you can live it. What is the noblest object of desire, the supreme gift to covet?

We have been accustomed to be told that the greatest thing in the religious world is Faith. That great word has been the keynote for centuries of the popular religion; and we have easily learned to look upon it as the greatest thing in the world. Well, we are wrong. If we have been told that, we may miss the mark. I have taken you in the chapter which I have just read, to Christianity at its source; and there we have seen, "The greatest of these is love." It is not an oversight. Paul was speaking of faith just a moment before. He says, "If I have all faith, so that I can remove mountains, and have not love; I am nothing." So far from forgetting he deliberately contrasts them, "Now abideth Faith, Hope, Love," and without a moment's hesitation the decision falls, "The greatest of these is Love."

And it is not prejudice. A man is apt to recommend to others his own strong point.

Love was not Paul's strong point. The observing student can detect a beautiful tenderness growing and ripening all through his character as Paul gets old; but the hand that wrote "The greatest of these is love," when we meet it first, is stained with blood.

Nor is this letter to the Corinthians peculiar in singling out love as the than *summum bonum*. The masterpieces of Christianity are agreed about it. Peter says, "Above all things have fervent love among yourselves." *Above all things*. And John goes farther, "God is love." And you remember the profound remark which Paul makes elsewhere, "Love is the fulfilling of the law." Did you ever think what he meant by that? In those days men were working their passage to Heaven by keeping the Ten Commandments, and the hundred and ten other commandments which they had manufactured out of them. Christ said, I will show you a more simple way. If you do one thing, you will do these hundred and ten things, without ever thinking about them. If you love, you will unconsciously fulfil the whole law. And you can readily see for yourselves how that must be so. Take any of the commandments. "Thou shalt have no other gods before Me." If a man love God, you will not require to tell him that. Love is the fulfilling of that law. "Take not His name in vain." Would he ever dream of taking His name in vain if he loved Him? "Remember the Sabbath day to keep it holy." Would he not be too glad to have one day in seven to dedicate more exclusively to the object of his affection? Love would fulfil all these laws regarding God. And so, if he loved Man you would never think of telling him to honor his father and mother. He could not do anything else. It would be preposterous to tell him not to kill. You could only insult him if you suggested that he should not steal—how could he steal from those he loved. It would be superfluous to beg him not to bear false witness against his neighbor. If he loved him it would be the last thing he would do.

And you would never dream of urging him not to covet what his neighbors had. He would rather they possessed it than himself. In this way "Love is the fulfilling of the law." It is the rule for fulfilling all rules, the new commandment for keeping all the old commandments, Christ's one secret of the Christian life.

Now Paul had learned that; and in this noble eulogy he has given us the most wonderful and original account extant of the *summum bonum*. We may divide it into three parts. In the beginning of the short chapter, we have Love *contrasted*; in the heart of it, we have Love *analyzed*; toward the end, we have Love *defended* as the supreme gift.

THE CONTRAST

Paul begins by contrasting Love with other things that men in those days thought much of. I shall not attempt to go over those things in detail. Their inferiority is already obvious.

He contrasts it with eloquence. And what a noble gift it is, the power of playing upon the souls and wills of men, and rousing them to lofty purposes and holy deeds. Paul says, "If I speak with the tongues of men and of angels, and have not love, I am become as sounding brass, or a tinkling cymbal." And we all know why. We have all felt the brazenness of words without emotion, the hollowness, the unaccountable unpersuasiveness, of eloquence behind which lies no Love.

He contrasts it with prophecy. He contrasts it with mysteries. He contrasts it with faith. He contrasts it with charity. Why is Love greater than faith? Because the end is greater than the means. And why is it greater than charity? Because the whole is greater than the part. Love is greater faith, because the end is greater than the means. What is the use of having faith? It is to connect the soul with God. And what is the object of connecting man with God? That he may become like God. But God is Love. Hence Faith, the means, is in order to Love, the end. Love, therefore, obviously is greater than faith. It is greater than charity, again, because the whole is greater than a part. Charity is only a little bit of Love, one of the innumerable avenues of Love, and there may even be, and there is, a great deal of charity without Love. It is a very easy thing to toss a copper to a beggar on the street; it is generally an easier thing than not to do it. Yet Love is just as often in the withholding. We purchase relief from the sympathetic feelings roused by the spectacle of misery, at the copper's cost. It is too cheap—too cheap for us, and often too dear for the beggar. If we really loved him we would either do more for him, or less.

Then Paul contrasts it with sacrifice and martyrdom. And I beg the little band of would-be missionaries—and I have the honor to call some of you by this name for the first time—to remember that though you give your bodies to be burned, and have not Love, it profits nothing—nothing! You can take nothing greater to the heathen world than the impress and the reflection of the Love of God upon your own character. That is the universal language. It will take you years to speak in Chinese, or in the dialects of India. From the day you land, that language of Love, understood by all, will be pouring forth its unconscious eloquence. It is the man who is the missionary, it is not his words. His character is his message. In the heart of Africa, among the great Lakes, I have come across black men and women who remembered the only white man they ever saw before—David Livingstone; and as you cross his footsteps in that dark continent, men's faces light up as they speak of the kind Doctor who passed there years ago. They could not understand him; but they felt the Love that beat in his heart. Take into your new sphere of labor, where you also mean to lay down your life, that simple charm, and your lifework must succeed. You can take nothing greater, you need take nothing less. It is not worth while going if you take anything less. You may take every accomplishment; you may be braced for every sacrifice; but if you give your body to be burned, and have not Love, it will profit you and the cause of Christ *nothing*.

THE ANALYSIS

After contrasting Love with these things, Paul, in three verses, very short, gives us an amazing analysis of what this supreme thing is. I ask you to look at it. It is a compound thing, he tells us. It is like light. As you have seen a man of science take a beam of light and pass it through a crystal prism, as you have seen it come out on the other side of the prism broken up into its component colors—red, and blue, and yellow, and violet, and orange, and all the colors of the rainbow—so Paul passes this thing, Love, through the magnificent prism of his inspired intellect, and it comes out on the other side broken up into its elements. And in these few words we have what one might call the Spectrum of Love, the analysis of Love. Will you observe what its elements are? Will you notice that they have common names; that they are virtues which we hear about every day; that they are things which can be practiced by every man in every place in life; and how, by a multitude of small things and ordinary virtues, the supreme thing, the *summum bonum*, is made up.

The Spectrum of Love has nine ingredients:

Patience—"Love suffereth long."
Kindness—"And is kind."
Generosity—"Love envieth not."
Humility—"Love vaunteth not itself, is not puffed up."
Courtesy—"Doth not behave itself unseemly."
Unselfishness—"Seeketh not her own."
Good Temper—"Is not easily provoked."
Guilelessness—"Thinketh no evil."
Sincerity—"Rejoiceth not in iniquity, but rejoiceth in the truth."

Patience; kindness; generosity; humility; courtesy; unselfishness; good temper; guilelessness; sincerity—these make up the supreme gift, the stature of the perfect man. You will observe that all are in relation to men, in relation to life, in relation to the known to-day and the near to-morrow, and not to the unknown eternity. We hear much of love to God; Christ spoke much of love to man. We make a great deal of peace with heaven; Christ made much of peace on earth. Religion is not a strange or added thing, but the inspiration of the secular life, the breathing of an eternal spirit through this temporal world. The supreme thing, in short, is not a thing at all, but the giving of a further finish to the multitudinous words and acts which make up the sum of every common day.

There is no time to do more than make a passing note upon each of these ingredients. Love is *Patience*. This is the normal attitude of Love; Love passive, Love waiting to begin; not in a hurry; calm; ready to do its work when the summons comes, but meantime wearing the ornament of a meek and quiet spirit. Love suffers long; beareth all things; believeth all things; hopeth all things. For love understands, and therefore waits.

Kindness. Love active. Have you ever noticed how much of Christ's life was spent in doing kind things—in *merely* doing kind things? Run over it with that in view, and you will find that He spent a great proportion of His time simply in making people happy, in doing good turns to people. There is only one thing greater than happiness in the world, and that is holiness; and it is not in our keeping; but what God *has* put in our power is the happiness of those about us, and that is largely to be secured by our being kind to them.

"The greatest thing," says some one, "a man can do for his Heavenly Father is to be kind to some of His other children." I wonder why it is that we are not all kinder than we are? How much the world needs it. How easily it is done. How instantaneously it acts. How infallibly it is remembered. How superabundantly it pays itself back—for there is no debtor in the world so honorable, so superbly honorable, as Love. "Love never faileth." Love is success, Love is happiness, Love is life. "Love I say," with Browning, "is energy of Life."

> For life, with all it yields of joy or woe
> And hope and fear,

Is just our chance o' the prize of learning love,—
How love might be, hath been indeed, and is.

Where Love is, God is. He that dwelleth in Love dwelleth in God. God is Love. Therefore *love*. Without distinction, without calculation, without procrastination, love. Lavish it upon the poor, where it is very easy; especially upon the rich, who often need it most; most of all upon our equals, where it is very difficult, and for whom perhaps we each do least of all. There is a difference between *trying to please* and *giving pleasure*. Give pleasure. Lose no chance of giving pleasure. For that is the ceaseless and anonymous triumph of a truly loving spirit. "I shall pass through this world but once. Any good thing therefore that I can do, or any kindness that I can show to any human being, let me do it now. Let me not defer it or neglect it, for I shall not pass this way again."

Generosity. "Love envieth not." This is love in competition with others. Whenever you attempt a good work you will find other men doing the same kind of work, and probably doing it better. Envy them not. Envy is a feeling of ill-will to those who are in the same line as ourselves, a spirit of covetousness and detraction. How little Christian work even is a protection against un-Christian feeling. That most despicable of all the unworthy moods which cloud a Christian's soul assuredly waits for us on the threshold of every work, unless we are fortified with this grace of magnanimity. Only one thing truly need the Christian envy, the large, rich, generous soul which "envieth not."

And then, after having learned all that, you have to learn this further thing, *Humility*—to put a seal upon your lips and forget what you have done. After you have been kind, after Love has stolen forth into the world and done its beautiful work, go back into the shade again and say nothing about it. Love hides even from itself. Love waives even self-satisfaction. "Love vaunteth not itself, is not puffed up."

The fifth ingredient is a somewhat strange one to find in this *summum bonum: Courtesy.* This is Love in society, Love in relation to etiquette. "Love doth not behave itself unseemly." Politeness has been defined as love in trifles. Courtesy is said to be love in little things. And the one secret of politeness is to love. Love *cannot* behave itself unseemly. You can put the most untutored persons into the highest society, and if they have a reservoir of Love in their heart, they will not behave themselves unseemly. They simply cannot do it. Carlyle said of Robert Burns that there was no truer gentleman in Europe than the ploughman-poet. It was because he loved everything— the mouse, and the daisy, and all the things, great and small, that God had made. So with this simple passport he could mingle with any society, and enter courts and palaces from his little cottage on the banks of the Ayr. You know the meaning of the word "gentleman." It means a gentle man—a man who does things gently with love. And that is the whole art and mystery of it. The gentleman cannot in the nature of things do an ungentle, and ungentlemanly thing. The ungentle soul, the inconsiderate, unsympathetic nature cannot do anything else. "Love doth not behave itself unseemly."

Unselfishness. "Love seeketh not her own." Observe: Seeketh not even that which is her own. In Britain the Englishman is devoted, and rightly, to his rights. But there come times when a man may exercise even the higher right of giving up his rights. Yet Paul does not summon us to give up our rights. Love strikes much deeper. It would have us not seek them at all, ignore them, eliminate the personal element altogether from our calculations. It is not hard to give up our rights. They are often external. The difficult thing is to give up ourselves. The more difficult thing still is not to seek things for ourselves at all. After we have sought them, bought them, won them, deserved them, we have taken the cream off them for ourselves already. Little cross then to give them up. But not to seek them, to look every man not on his own things, but on the things of others—*id opus est.* "Seekest thou great things for thyself?" said the prophet; "*seek them not.*" Why? Because there is no greatness in *things*. Things cannot be great. The only greatness is unselfish love. Even self-denial in itself is nothing, is almost a mistake. Only a great purpose or a mightier love can justify the waste. It is more difficult, I have said, not to seek our own at all, than, having sought it, to give it up. I must take that back. It is only true of a partly selfish heart. Nothing is a hardship to Love, and nothing is hard. I believe that Christ's "yoke" is easy. Christ's "yoke" is just His way of taking life. And I believe it is an easier way than any other. I believe it is a happier way than any other. The most obvious lesson in Christ's teaching is that there is no happiness in having and getting anything, but only in giving. I repeat, *there is no happiness in having or in getting, but only in giving.* And half the world is on the wrong scent in pursuit of happiness. They think it consists in having and getting, and in being served by others. It consists in giving, and in serving others. He that would be great among you, said Christ, let him serve.

He that would be happy, let him remember that there is but one way—it is more blessed, it is more happy, to give than to receive.

The next ingredient is a very remarkable one: *Good Temper*. "Love is not easily provoked." Nothing could be more striking than to find this here. We are inclined to look upon bad temper as a very harmless weakness. We speak of it as a mere infirmity of nature, a family failing, a matter of temperament, not a thing to take into very serious account in estimating a man's character. And yet here, right in the heart of this analysis of love, it finds a place; and the Bible again and again returns to condemn it as one of the most destructive elements in human nature.

The peculiarity of ill temper is that it is the vice of the virtuous. It is often the one blot on an otherwise noble character. You know men who are all but perfect, and women who would be entirely perfect, but for an easily ruffled, quick-tempered, or "touchy" disposition. This compatibility of ill temper with high moral character is one of the strangest and saddest problems of ethics. The truth is there are two great classes of sins—sins of the *Body*, and sins of the *Disposition*. The Prodigal Son may be taken as a type of the first, the Elder Brother of the second. Now, society has no doubt whatever as to which of these is the worse. Its brand falls, without a challenge, upon the Prodigal. But are we right? We have no balance to weigh one another's sins, and coarser and finer are but human words; but faults in the higher nature may be less venial than those in the lower, and to the eye of Him who is Love, a sin against Love may seem a hundred times more base. No form of vice, not worldliness, not greed of gold, not drunkenness itself, does more to un-Christianize society than evil temper. For embittering life, for breaking up communities, for destroying the most sacred relationships, for devastating homes, for withering up men and women, for taking the bloom of childhood, in short, for sheer gratuitous misery-producing power, this influence stands alone. Look at the Elder Brother, moral, hard-working, patient, dutiful—let him get all credit for his virtues—look at this man, this baby, sulking outside his own father's door. "He was angry," we read, "and would not go in." Look at the effect upon the father, upon the servants, upon the happiness of the guests. Judge of the effect upon the Prodigal—and how many prodigals are kept out of the Kingdom of God by the unlovely character of those who profess to be inside? Analyze, as a study in Temper, the thunder-cloud as it gathers upon the Elder-Brother's brow. What is it made of? Jealousy, anger, pride, uncharity, cruelty, self-righteousness, touchiness, doggedness, sullenness,— these are the ingredients of this dark and loveless soul. In varying proportions, also, these are the ingredients of all ill temper. Judge if such sins of the disposition are not worse to live in, and for others to live with, than sins of the body. Did Christ indeed not answer the question Himself when He said, "I say unto you, that the publicans and the harlots go into the Kingdom of Heaven before you"? There is really no place in Heaven for a disposition like this. A man with such a mood could only make Heaven miserable for all the people in it. Except, therefore, such a man be born again, he cannot, he simply *cannot*, enter the Kingdom of Heaven. For it is perfectly certain—and you will not misunderstand me—that to enter Heaven a man must take it with him.

You will see then why Temper is significant. It is not in what it is alone, but in what it reveals. This is why I take the liberty now of speaking of it with such unusual plainness. It is a test for love, a symptom, a revelation of an unloving nature at bottom. It is the intermittent fever which bespeaks unintermittent disease within; the occasional bubble escaping to the surface which betrays some rottenness underneath; a sample of the most hidden products of the soul dropped involuntarily when off one's guard; in a word, the lightning form of a hundred hideous and un-Christian sins. For a want of patience, a want of kindness, a want of generosity, a want of courtesy, a want of unselfishness, all are instantaneously symbolized in one flash of Temper.

Hence it is not enough to deal with the Temper. We must go to the source, and change the inmost nature, and the angry humors will die away of themselves. Souls are made sweet not by taking the acid fluids out, but by putting something in—a great Love, a new Spirit, the Spirit of Christ. Christ, the Spirit of Christ, interpenetrating ours, sweetens, purifies, transforms all. This only can eradicate what is wrong, work a chemical change, renovate and regenerate, and rehabilitate the inner man. Will-power does not change men. Time does not change men. Christ does. Therefore "Let that mind be in you which was also in Christ Jesus." Some of us have not much time to lose. Remember, once more, that this is a matter of life or death. I cannot help speaking urgently, for myself, for yourselves. "Whoso shall offend one of these little ones, which believe in me, it were better for him that a millstone were hanged about his neck, and that he were drowned in the depth of the sea." That is to say, it is the deliberate verdict of the Lord Jesus that it is better not to live than not to love. *It is better not to live than not to love.*

Guilelessness and *Sincerity* may be dismissed almost with a word. Guilelessness is the grace for suspicious people. And the possession of it is the great secret of personal influence. You will find, if you think for a moment, that the people who influence you are people who believe in you. In an atmosphere of suspicion men shrivel up; but in that atmosphere they expand, and find encouragement and educative fellowship. It is a wonderful thing that here and there in this hard, uncharitable world there should still be left a few rare souls who think no evil. This is the great unworldliness. Love "Thinketh no evil," imputes no motive, sees the bright side, puts the best construction on every action. What a delightful state of mind to live in! What a stimulus and benediction even to meet with it for a day! To be trusted is to be saved. And if we try to influence or elevate others, we shall soon see that success is in proportion to their belief of our belief in them. For the respect of another is the first restoration of the self-respect a man has lost; our ideal of what he is becomes to him the hope and pattern of what he may become.

"Love rejoiceth not in iniquity, but rejoiceth in the truth." I have called this *Sincerity* from the words rendered in the Authorized Version by "rejoiceth in the truth." And certainly, were this the real translation, nothing could be more just. For he who loves will love Truth not less than men. He will rejoice in the Truth—rejoice not in what he has been taught to believe; not in this Church's doctrine or in that; not in this ism or in that ism; but "in *the Truth*." He will accept only what is real; he will strive to get at facts; he will search for *Truth* with a humble and unbiassed mind, and cherish whatever he finds at any sacrifice. But the more literal translation of the Revised Version calls for just such a sacrifice for truth's sake here. For what Paul really meant is, as we there read, "Rejoiceth not in unrighteousness, but rejoiceth with the truth," a quality which probably no one English word—and certainly not *Sincerity*—adequately defines. It includes, perhaps more strictly, the self-restraint which refuses to make capital out of others' faults; the charity which delights not in exposing the weakness of others, but "covereth all things"; the sincerity of purpose which endeavors to see things as they are, and rejoices to find them better than suspicion feared or calumny denounced.

So much for the analysis of Love. Now the business of our lives is to have these things fitted into our characters. That is the supreme work to which we need to address ourselves in this world, to learn Love. Is life not full of opportunities for learning Love? Every man and woman every day has a thousand of them. The world is not a playground; it is a schoolroom. Life is not a holiday, but an education. And the one eternal lesson for us all is *how better we can love*. What makes a man a good cricketer? Practice. What makes a man a good artist, a good sculptor, a good musician? Practice. What makes a man a good linguist, a good stenographer? Practice. What makes a man a good man? Practice. Nothing else. There is nothing capricious about religion. We do not get the soul in different ways, under different laws, from those in which we get the body and the mind. If a man does not exercise his arm he develops no biceps muscle; and if a man does not exercise his soul, he acquires no muscle in his soul, no strength of character, no vigor of moral fibre, nor beauty of spiritual growth. Love is not a thing of enthusiastic emotion. It is a rich, strong, manly, vigorous expression of the whole round Christian character—the Christlike nature in its fullest development. And the constituents of this great character are only to be built up by ceaseless practice.

What was Christ doing in the carpenter's shop? Practicing. Though perfect, we read that He *learned* obedience, and grew in wisdom and in favor with God. Do not quarrel therefore with your lot in life. Do not complain of its never ceasing cares, its petty environment, the vexations you have to stand, the small and sordid souls you have to live and work with. Above all, do not resent temptation; do not be perplexed because it seems to thicken round you more and more, and ceases neither for effort nor for agony nor prayer. That is your practice. That is the practice which God appoints you; and it is having its work in making you patient, and humble, and generous, and unselfish, and kind, and courteous. Do not grudge the hand that is moulding the still too shapeless image within you. It is growing more beautiful, though you see it not, and every touch of temptation may add to its perfection. Therefore keep in the midst of life. Do not isolate yourself. Be among men, and among things, and among troubles, and difficulties, and obstacles. You remember Goethe's words: *Es bildet ein Talent sich in der Stille, Doch ein Charakter in dem Strom der Welt.* "Talent develops itself in solitude; character in the stream of life." Talent develops itself in solitude—the talent of prayer, of faith, of meditation, of seeing the unseen; Character grows in the stream of the world's life. That chiefly is where men are to learn love.

How? Now, how? To make it easier, I have named a few of the elements of love. But these are only elements. Love itself can never be defined. Light is a something more than the sum of its ingredients—a glowing, dazzling, tremulous ether. And love is something more than all its elements—a palpitating, quivering, sensitive, living thing. By synthesis of all the colors, men can make whiteness, they cannot make light. By synthesis of all the virtues, men can make virtue, they cannot make love. How then are we to have this transcendent living whole conveyed into our souls? We brace our wills to secure it. We try to copy those who have it. We lay down rules about it. We watch. We pray. But these things alone will not bring Love into our nature. Love is an *effect*. And only as we fulfil the right condition can we have the effect produced. Shall I tell you what the *cause* is?

If you turn to the Revised Version of the First Epistle of John you will find these words: "We love because He first loved us." "We love," not "We love *Him*." That is the way the old version has it, and it is quite wrong. "*We love*—because He first loved us." Look at that word "because." It is the *cause* of which I have spoken. "*Because* He first loved us," the effect follows that we love, we love Him, we love all men. We cannot help it. Because He loved us, we love, we love everybody. Our heart is slowly changed. Contemplate the love of Christ, and you will love. Stand before that mirror, reflect Christ's character and you will be changed into the same image from tenderness to tenderness. There is no other way. You cannot love to order. You can only look at the lovely object, and fall in love with it, and grow into likeness to it. And so look at this Perfect Character, this Perfect Life. Look at the great Sacrifice as He laid down Himself, all through life, and

19

upon the Cross of Calvary, and you must love Him. And loving Him, you must become like Him. Love begets love. It is a process of induction. Put a piece of iron in the presence of an electrified body, and that piece of iron for a time becomes electrified. It is changed into a temporary magnet in the mere presence of a permanent magnet, and as long as you leave the two side by side, they are both magnets alike. Remain side by side with Him who loved us, and gave Himself for us, and you too will become a permanent magnet, a permanently attractive force; and like Him you will draw all men unto you, like Him you will be drawn unto all men. That is the inevitable effect of Love. Any man who fulfils that cause must have that effect produced in him. Try to give up the idea that religion comes to us by chance, or by mystery, or by caprice. It comes to us by natural law, or by supernatural law, for all law is Divine. Edward Irving went to see a dying boy once, and when he entered the room he just put his hand on the sufferer's head, and said, "My boy, God loves you," and went away. And the boy started from his bed, and called out to the people in the house, "God loves me! God loves me!" It changed that boy. The sense that God loved him overpowered him, melted him down, and began the creating of a new heart in him. And that is how the love of God melts down the unlovely heart in man, and begets in him the new creature, who is patient and humble and gentle and unselfish. And there is no other way to get it. There is no mystery about it. We love others, we love everybody, we love our enemies, because He first loved us.

THE DEFENCE

Now I have a closing sentence or two to add about Paul's reason for singling out love as the supreme possession. It is a very remarkable reason. In a single word it is this: *it lasts*. "Love," urges Paul, "never faileth." Then he begins again one of his marvellous lists of the great things of the day, and exposes them one by one. He runs over the things that men thought were going to last, and shows that they are all fleeting, temporary, passing away.

"Whether there be prophecies, they shall fail." It was the mother's ambition for her boy in those days that he should become a prophet. For hundreds of years God had never spoken by means of any prophet, and at that time the prophet was greater than the King. Men waited wistfully for another messenger to come and hung upon his lips when he appeared as upon the very voice of God. Paul says, "Whether there be prophecies, they shall fail." This book is full of prophecies. One by one they have "failed"; that is, having been fulfilled, their work is finished; they have nothing more to do now in the world except to feed a devout man's faith.

Then Paul talks about tongues. That was another thing that was greatly coveted. "Whether there be tongues, they shall cease." As we all know, many, many centuries have passed since tongues have been known in this world. They have ceased. Take it in any sense you like. Take it, for illustration merely, as languages in general—a sense which was not in Paul's mind at all, and which though it cannot give us the specific lesson will point the general truth. Consider the words in which these chapters were written— Greek. It has gone. Take the Latin—the other great tongue of those days. It ceased long ago. Look at the Indian language. It is ceasing. The language of Wales, of Ireland, of the Scottish Highlands, is dying before our eyes. The most popular book in the English tongue at the present time, except the Bible, is one of Dickens's works, his *Pickwick Papers*. It is largely written in the language of London street-life; and experts assure us that in fifty years it will be unintelligible to the average English reader.

Then Paul goes farther, and with even greater boldness adds, "Whether there be knowledge, it shall vanish away." The wisdom of the ancients, where is it? It is wholly gone. A schoolboy to-day knows more than Sir Isaac Newton knew. His knowledge has vanished away. You put yesterday's newspaper in the fire. Its knowledge has vanished away. You buy the old editions of the great encyclopaedias for a few pence. Their knowledge has vanished away. Look how the coach has been superseded by the use of steam. Look how electricity has superseded that, and swept a hundred almost new inventions into oblivion. One of the greatest living authorities, Sir William Thomson, said the other day, "The steam-engine is passing away." "Whether there be knowledge, it shall vanish away." At every workshop you will see, in a back yard, a heap of old iron, a few wheels, a few levers, a few cranks, broken and eaten with rust. Twenty years ago that was the pride of the city. Men flocked in from the country to see the great invention; now it is superseded, its day is done. And all the boasted science and philosophy of this day will soon be old. But yesterday, in the University of Edinburgh, the greatest figure in the faculty was Sir James Simpson, the discoverer of chloroform. The other day his successor and nephew, Professor Simpson, was asked by the librarian of the University to go to the library and pick out the books on his subject that were no longer needed. And his reply to the librarian was this: "Take every text-book that is more than ten years old, and put it down in the cellar." Sir James Simpson was a great authority only a few years ago: men came from all parts of the earth to consult him; and almost the whole teaching of that time is consigned by the science of to-day to oblivion. And in every branch of science it is the same. "Now we know in part. We see through a glass darkly."

Can you tell me anything that is going to last? Many things Paul did not condescend to name. He did not mention money, fortune, fame; but he picked out the great things of his time, the things the best men thought had something in them, and brushed them peremptorily aside. Paul had no charge against these things in themselves. All he said about them was that they would not last. They were great things, but not supreme things. There were things beyond them. What we are stretches past what we do, beyond what we possess. Many things that men denounce as sins are not sins; but they are temporary. And that is a favorite argument of the New Testament. John says of the world, not that it is wrong, but simply that it "passeth away." There is a great deal in the world that is delightful and beautiful; there is a great deal in it that is great and engrossing; but it will not last. All that is in the world, the lust of the eye, the lust of the flesh, and the pride of life, are but for a little while. Love not the world therefore. Nothing that it contains is worth the life and consecration of an immortal soul. The immortal soul must give itself to something that is immortal. And the only immortal things are these: "Now abideth faith, hope, love, but the greatest of these is love."

Some think the time may come when two of these three things will also pass away—faith into sight, hope into fruition. Paul does not say so. We know but little now about the conditions of the life that is to come. But what is certain is that Love must last. God, the Eternal God, is Love. Covet therefore that everlasting gift, that one thing which it is certain is going to stand, that one coinage which will be current in the Universe when all the other coinages of all the nations of the world shall be useless and unhonored. You will give yourselves to many things, give yourself first to Love. Hold things in their proportion. *Hold things in their proportion.* Let at least the first great object of our lives be to achieve the character defended in these words, the character—and it is the character of Christ—which is built round Love.

I have said this thing is eternal. Did you ever notice how continually John associates love and faith with eternal life? I was not told when I was a boy that "God so loved the world that He gave His only-begotten Son, that whosoever believeth in Him should have everlasting life." What I was told, I remember, was, that God so loved the world that, if I trusted in Him, I was to have a thing called peace, or I was to have rest, or I was to have joy, or I was to have safety. But I had to find out for myself that whosoever trusteth in Him—that is, whosoever loveth Him, for trust is only the avenue to Love—hath everlasting *life*. The Gospel offers a man life. Never offer men a thimbleful of Gospel. Do not offer them merely joy, or merely peace, or merely rest, or merely safety; tell them how Christ came to give men a more abundant life than they have, a life abundant in love, and therefore abundant in salvation for themselves, and large in enterprise for the alleviation

24

and redemption of the world. Then only can the Gospel take hold of the whole of a man, body, soul, and spirit, and give to each part of his nature its exercise and reward. Many of the current Gospels are addressed only to a part of man's nature. They offer peace, not life; faith, not Love; justification, not regeneration. And men slip back again from such religion because it has never really held them. Their nature was not all in it. It offered no deeper and gladder life-current than the life that was lived before. Surely it stands to reason that only a fuller love can compete with the love of the world.

To love abundantly is to live abundantly, and to love forever is to live forever. Hence, eternal life is inextricably bound up with love. We want to live forever for the same reason that we want to live to-morrow. Why do you want to live to-morrow? It is because there is some one who loves you, and whom you want to see to-morrow, and be with, and love back. There is no other reason why we should live on than that we love and are beloved. It is when a man has no one to love him that he commits suicide. So long as he has friends, those who love him and whom he loves, he will live, because to live is to love. Be it but the love of a dog, it will keep him in life; but let that go and he has no contact with life, no reason to live. He dies by his own hand. Eternal life also is to know God, and God is love. This is Christ's own definition. Ponder it. "This is life eternal, that they might know Thee the only true God, and Jesus Christ whom Thou hast sent." Love must be eternal. It is what God is. On the last analysis, then, love is life. Love never faileth, and life never faileth, so long as there is love. That is the philosophy of what Paul is showing us; the reason why in the nature of things Love should be the supreme thing—because it is going to last;

because in the nature of things it is an Eternal Life. It is a thing that we are living now, not that we get when we die; that we shall have a poor chance of getting when we die unless we are living now. No worse fate can befall a man in this world than to live and grow old alone, unloving and unloved. To be lost is to live in an unregenerate condition, loveless and unloved; and to be saved is to love; and he that dwelleth in love dwelleth already in God. For God is Love.

Now I have all but finished. How many of you will join me in reading this chapter once a week for the next three months? A man did that once and it changed his whole life. Will you do it? It is for the greatest thing in the world. You might begin by reading it every day, especially the verses which describe the perfect character. "Love suffereth long, and is kind; love envieth not; love vaunteth not itself." Get these ingredients into your life. Then everything that you do is eternal. It is worth doing. It is worth giving time to. No man can become a saint in his sleep; and to fulfil the condition required demands a certain amount of prayer and meditation and time, just as improvement in any direction, bodily or mental, requires preparation and care. Address yourselves to that one thing; at any cost have this transcendent character exchanged for yours. You will find as you look back upon your life that the moments that stand out, the moments when you have really lived, are the moments when you have done things in a spirit of love. As memory scans the past, above and beyond all the transitory pleasures of life, there leap forward those supreme hours when you have been enabled to do unnoticed kindnesses to those round about you, things too trifling to speak about, but which you feel have entered into your eternal life. I have seen almost all the beautiful things God has made; I have enjoyed almost every pleasure that He has planned for man; and yet as I look back I see standing out above all the life that has gone four or five short experiences when the love of God reflected itself in some poor imitation, some small act of love of mine, and these seem to be the things which alone of all one's life abide. Everything else in all our lives is transitory. Every other good is visionary. But the acts of love which no man knows about, or can ever know about—they never fail.

In the book of Matthew, where the Judgment Day is depicted for us in the imagery of One seated upon a throne and dividing the sheep from the goats, the test of a man then is not, "How have I believed?" but "How have I loved?" The test of religion, the final test of religion, is not religiousness but Love. I say the final test of religion at that great Day is not religiousness, but Love; not what I have done, not what I have believed, not what I have achieved, but how I have discharged the common charities of life. Sins of commission in that awful indictment are not even referred to. By what we have not done, *by sins of omission*, we are judged. It could not be otherwise. For the withholding of love is the negation of the spirit of Christ, the proof that we never knew Him, that for us He lived in vain. It means that He suggested nothing in all our thoughts, that He inspired nothing in all our lives, that we were not once near enough to Him to be seized with the spell of His compassion for the world. It means that—

I lived for myself, I thought for myself,
For myself, and none beside—
Just as if Jesus had never lived,
As if He had never died.

It is the Son of *Man* before whom the nations of the world shall be gathered. It is in the presence of *Humanity* that we shall be charged. And the spectacle itself, the mere sight of it, will silently judge each one. Those will be there whom we have met and helped; or there, the unpitied multitude whom we neglected or despised. No other Witness need be summoned. No other charge than lovelessness shall be preferred. Be not deceived. The words which all of us shall one Day hear sound not of theology but of life, not of churches and saints but of the hungry and the poor, not of creeds and doctrines but of shelter and clothing, not of Bibles and prayer-books but of cups of cold water in the name of Christ. Thank God the Christianity of to-day is coming nearer the world's need. Live to help that on. Thank God men know better, by a hair's-breadth, what religion is, what God is, who Christ is, where Christ is. Who is Christ? He who fed the hungry, clothed the naked, visited the sick. And where is Christ? Where?— whoso shall receive a little child in My name receiveth Me. And who are Christ's? Every one that loveth is born of God.

The Autobiography of Benjamin Franklin is one of my favorite books. My mother recommended it to me when I was young. And I have reread it regularly ever since.

In its sixth chapter Franklin undertakes to improve his character and rid himself of his faults. He goes about doing so with a scientific method that could be a model for anyone.

I have tried it myself and it works. Of course, I have not attained perfect results, but I assure you it is worth diligent persistence. In reading this chapter of Franklin's life story, we get a clue to his success and enduring wisdom. It provides an insight into the mind of one of our greatest Americans. I have condensed the chapter, but Franklin's method of self-improvement is there, and trying it will enhance your life.

From "The Autobiography of Benjamin Franklin"
(1706–1790)

AT THE TIME I established myself in Pennsylvania, there was not a good bookseller's shop in any of the colonies to the southward of Boston. In New York and Philadelphia the printers were indeed stationers, but they sold only paper, almanacs, ballads, and a few common school-books. Those who loved reading were obliged to send for their books from England. Some did this and a club was formed, a room hired where we could all bring our books, be ready to consult in our conferences, but of a more common benefit, each of us were at liberty to borrow any book he wished to read at home. This was accordingly done, and for some time contented us.

Finding the advantage of this little collection, I proposed to render the benefit from the books more common, by commencing a public subscription library. I drew a sketch of the plan and rules that would be necessary, and got a skillful conveyancer, Mr. Charles Brockden, to put the whole in form of articles of agreement to be subscribed, by which each subscriber engaged to pay a certain sum down for the first purchase of the books, and an annual contribution for increasing them.

So few were the readers at that time in Philadelphia, and the majority of us so poor, that I was not able, with great industry, to find more than fifty persons, mostly young tradesmen, willing to pay down for this purpose forty shillings each, and ten shillings per annum. With this little fund we began.

The books were imported; the library was opened one day in the week for lending them to the subscribers, on their promissory notes to pay double the value, if not duly returned. The institution soon manifested its utility, was imitated by other towns, and in other provinces. The libraries were augmented by donations; reading became fashionable; and our people, having no public amusements to divert their attention from study, became better acquainted with books, and in a few years were observed by strangers to be better instructed and more intelligent than people of the same rank generally are in other countries.

When we were about to sign the above-mentioned articles, which were to be binding on us, our heirs, &c., for fifty years, Mr. Brockden, the scrivener, said to us, "You are young men, but it is scarcely probable that any of you will live to see the expiration of the term fixed in the instrument." A number of us, however, are yet living; but the instrument was after a few years rendered null by a charter that incorporated and gave perpetuity to the company.

The objections and reluctances I met with in soliciting the subscriptions, made me soon feel the impropriety of presenting one's self as the proposer of any useful project, that might be supposed to raise one's reputation in the smallest degree above that of one's neighbors, when one has need of their assistance to accomplish that project. I therefore put myself as much as I could out of sight, and stated it as a scheme of a *number of friends*, who had requested me to go about and propose it to such as they thought lovers of reading. In this way my affair went on more smoothly, and I ever after practiced it on such occasions; and, from my frequent successes, can heartily recommend it. The present little sacrifice of your vanity will afterward be amply repaid. If it remains a while uncertain to whom the merit belongs, some one more vain than yourself may be encouraged to claim it.

This library afforded me the means of improvement by constant study, for which I set apart an hour or two each day, and thus repaired in some degree the loss of the learned education my father once intended for me. Reading was the only amusement I allowed myself. I spent no time in taverns, games, or frolics of any kind; and my industry in my business continued as indefatigable as it was necessary. I was indebted for my printing-house; I had a young family coming on to be educated, and I had two competitors to contend with for business, who were established in the place before me.

My circumstances, however, grew daily easier. My original habits of frugality continuing, and my father having, among his instructions to me when a boy, frequently repeated a proverb of Solomon, "*Seest thou a man diligent in his calling, he shall stand before kings, he shall not stand before mean men,*" I thence considered industry as a means of obtaining wealth and distinction, which encouraged me, though I did not think that I should ever literally *stand before kings,* which, however, has since happened; for I have stood before *five,* and even had the honor of sitting down with one, the King of Denmark, to dinner.

We have an English proverb that says, "*He that would thrive, must ask his wife.*" It was lucky for me that I had one as much disposed to industry and frugality as myself. She assisted me cheerfully in my business, folding and stitching pamphlets, tending shop, purchasing old linen rags for the paper makers, &c. We kept no idle servants, our table was plain and simple, our furniture of the cheapest. For instance, my breakfast was for a long time bread and milk (no tea), and I ate it out of a two penny earthen porringer, with a pewter spoon.

But mark how luxury will enter families, and make a progress, in spite of principle: being called one morning to breakfast, I found it in a China bowl, with a spoon of silver! They had been bought for me without my knowledge by my wife, and had cost her the enormous sum of three-and-twenty shillings, for which she had no other excuse or apology to make, but that she thought *her* husband deserved a silver spoon and China bowl as well as any of his neighbors. This was the first appearance of plate and China in our house, which afterward, in a course of years, as our wealth increased, augmented gradually to several hundred pounds in value.

I had been religiously educated as a Presbyterian; but, though some of the dogmas of that persuasion, such as *the eternal decrees of God, election, reprobation, &c.*, appearing to me unintelligible, others doubtful, and I early absented myself from the public assemblies of the sect, Sunday being my studying day, I never was without some religious principles. I never doubted, for instance, the existence of a Deity; that he made the world, and governed it by his providence; that the most acceptable service of God was the doing good to man; that our souls are immortal; and that all crimes will be punished, and virtue rewarded, either here or hereafter.

Though I seldom attended any public worship, I had still an opinion of its propriety, and of its utility when rightly conducted, and I regularly paid my annual subscription for the support of the only Presbyterian minister or meeting we had in Philadelphia. He used to visit me sometimes as a friend, and admonish me to attend his administrations, and I was now and then prevailed on to do so, once for five Sundays successively.

Had he been in my opinion a good preacher, perhaps I might have continued, notwithstanding the occasion I had for the Sunday's leisure in my course of study; but his discourses were chiefly either polemic arguments, or explications of the peculiar doctrines of our sect, and were all to me very dry, uninteresting, and unedifying, since not a single moral principle was inculcated or enforced, their aim seeming to be rather to make *us Presbyterians* than *good citizens*.

At length he took for his text that verse of the fourth chapter to the Philippians, "*Finally, brethren, whatsoever things are true, honest, just, pure, lovely, or of good report, if there be any virtue, or any praise, think on these things.*" And I imagined, in a sermon on such a text, we could not miss of having some morality. But he confined himself to five points only, as meant by the apostle: 1. Keeping holy the Sabbath day. 2. Being diligent in reading the holy Scriptures. 3. Attending duly the public worship. 4. Partaking of the Sacrament. 5. Paying a due respect to God's ministers. These might be all good things; but, as they were not the kind of good things that I expected from the text, I despaired of ever meeting with them from any other, was disgusted, and attended his preaching no more. I had some years before composed a little Liturgy, or form of prayer, for my own private use (in 1728), entitled, *Articles of Belief and Acts of Religion*. I returned to the use of this, and went no more to the public assemblies. My conduct might be blamable, but I leave it, without attempting further to excuse it; my present purpose being to relate facts, and not to make apologies for them.

It was about this time I conceived the bold and arduous project of arriving at *moral perfection*. I wished to live without committing any fault at any time, and to conquer all that either natural inclination, custom, or company might lead me into. As I knew, or thought I knew, what was right and wrong, I did not see why I might not *always* do the one and avoid the other. But I soon found I had undertaken a task of more difficulty than I had imagined. While my attention was taken up, and employed in guarding against one fault, I was often surprised by another; habit took the advantage of inattention; inclination was sometimes too strong for reason. I concluded, at length, that the mere speculative conviction that it was our interest to be completely virtuous, was not sufficient to prevent our slipping; and that the contrary habits must be broken, and good ones acquired and established, before we can have any dependence on a steady, uniform rectitude of conduct. For this purpose I therefore tried the following method.

In the various enumerations of the *moral virtues* I had met with in my reading, I found the catalogue more or less numerous, as different writers included more or fewer ideas under the same name. *Temperance*, for example, was by some confined to eating and drinking, while by others it was extended to mean the moderating every other pleasure, appetite, inclination, or passion, bodily or mental, even to our avarice and ambition. I proposed to myself, for the sake of clearness, to use rather more names, with fewer ideas annexed to each, than a few names with more ideas; and I included under thirteen names of virtues all that at that time occurred to me as necessary or desirable, and annexed to each a short precept, which fully expressed the extent I gave to its meaning.

These names of *virtues*, with their precepts, were,

1. *Temperance*. Eat not to dullness; drink not to elevation.
2. *Silence*. Speak not but what may benefit others or yourself; avoid trifling conversation.
3. *Order*. Let all your things have their places; let each part of your business have its time.
4. *Resolution*. Resolve to perform what you ought; perform without fail what you resolve.
5. *Frugality*. Make no expense but to do good to others or yourself; that is, waste nothing.

6. *Industry*. Lose no time; be always employed in something useful; cut off all unnecessary actions.

7. *Sincerity*. Use no hurtful deceit; think innocently and justly; and, if you speak, speak accordingly.

8. *Justice*. Wrong none by doing injuries, or omitting the benefits that are your duty.

9. *Moderation*. Avoid extremes; forbear resenting injuries so much as you think they deserve.

10. *Cleanliness*. Tolerate no uncleanliness in body, clothes, or habitation.

11. *Tranquility*. Be not disturbed at trifles, or at accidents common or unavoidable.

12. *Chastity*. . . .

13. *Humility*. Imitate Jesus and Socrates.

My intention being to acquire and *habitude* of all these virtues, I judged it would be well not to distract my attention by attempting the whole at once, but to fit it on *one* of them at a time; and, when I should be master of that, then to proceed to another, and so on, till I should have gone through the thirteen; and, as the previous acquisition of some might facilitate the acquisition of certain others, I arranged them with that view, as they stand above. *Temperance* first, as it tends to procure that coolness and clearness of head, which is so necessary where constant vigilance was to be kept up, and a guard maintained against the unremitting attraction of ancient habits, and the force of perpetual temptations.

This being acquired and established, *Silence* would be more easy; and my desire being to gain knowledge at the same time that I improved in virtue, and considering that in conversation it was obtained rather by the use of the ear than of the tongue, and therefore wishing to break a habit I was getting into of prattling, punning, and jesting, which only made me acceptable to trifling company, I gave *Silence* the second place.

This and the next, *Order,* I expected would allow me more time for attending to my project and my studies. *Resolution,* once become habitual, would keep me firm in my endeavors to obtain all the subsequent virtues; *Frugality* and *Industry* relieving me from my remaining debt, and producing affluence and independence, would make more easy the practice of *Sincerity* and *Justice,* &c., &c. Conceiving then, that, agreeably to the advice of Pythagoras in his *Golden Verses,* daily examination would be necessary, I contrived the following method for conducting that examination.

I made a little book, in which I allotted a page for each of the virtues. I ruled each page with red ink, so as to have seven columns, one for each day of the week, marking each column with a letter for the day. I crossed these columns with thirteen red lines, marking the beginning of each line with the first letter of one of the virtues, on which line, and in its proper column, I might mark, by a little black spot, every fault I found upon examination to have been committed respecting that virtue upon that day.[1]

I determined to give a week's strict attention to each of the virtues successively. Thus, in the first week, my great guard was to avoid every least of-

---

1. This "title book" is dated 1st July, 1733.

Form of the pages.

TEMPERANCE

Eat not to dullness; drink not to elevation.

	Sun.	M.	T.	W.	Th.	F.	S.
Tem.							
Sil.	*	*		*		*	
Ord.	*	*			*	*	*
Res.		*				*	
Fru.		*				*	
Ind.			*				
Sinc.							
Jus.							
Mod.							
Clea.							
Tran.							
Chas.							
Hum.							

fense against *Temperance*, leaving the other virtues to their ordinary chance, only marking every evening the faults of the day. Thus, if in the first week I could keep my first line, marked T, clear of spots, I supposed the habit of that virtue so much strengthened, and its opposite weakened, that I might venture extending my attention to include the next, and for the following week keep both lines clear of spots.

Proceeding thus to the last, I could get through a course complete in thirteen weeks, and four courses in a year. And like him who, having a garden to weed, does not attempt to eradicate all the bad herbs at once, which would exceed his reach and his strength, but works on one of the beds at a time, and, having accomplished the first, proceeds to a second, so I should have, I hoped, the encouraging pleasure of seeing on my pages the progress made in virtue, by clearing successively my lines of their spots, till in the end, by a number of courses, I should be happy in viewing a clean look, after a thirteen weeks' daily examination.

And conceiving God to be the fountain of wisdom, I thought it right and necessary to solicit his assistance for obtaining it; to this end I formed the following little prayer, which was prefixed to my tables of examination, for daily use.

> O powerful Goodness! bountiful Father! merciful Guide! Increase in me that wisdom which discovers my truest interest. Strengthen my resolution to perform what that wisdom dictates. Accept my kind offices to thy other children as the only return in my power for thy continual favors to me.

I used also sometimes a little prayer which I took from Thomson's *Poems*, viz.:

Father of light and life, thou Good Supreme!
O teach me what is good; teach me Thyself!
Save me from folly, vanity, and vice,
From every low pursuit; and feed my soul
With knowledge, conscious peace, and virtue pure;
Sacred, substantial, never-fading bliss!

The precept of *Order* requiring that *every part of my business should have its allotted time*, one page in my little book contained a scheme of employment for the twenty-four hours of a natural day.

I entered upon the execution of this plan for self-examination, and continued it with occasional intermissions for some time. I was surprised to find myself so much fuller of faults than I had imagined; but I had the satisfaction of seeing them diminish.

Because of my many faults, my scheme of *Order* gave me the most trouble; and I found that, though it might be practicable where a man's business was such as to leave him the disposition of his time, that of a journeyman printer, for instance, it was not possible to be exactly observed by a master, who must mix with the world, and often receive people of business at their own hours.

Order, too, with regard to places for things, papers, &c., I found extremely difficult to acquire. I had not been early accustomed to *method*, and, having an exceedingly good memory, I was not so sensible of the inconvenience attending want of method. This article, therefore, cost me much painful attention, and my faults in it vexed me so much, and I made so little progress in amendment, and had such frequent relapses, that I was almost ready to give up the attempt, and content myself with a faulty character in that respect, like the man who, in buying an ax of a smith, my neighbor, desired to have the whole of its surface as bright as the edge.

The smith consented to grind it bright for him if he would turn the wheel; he turned, while the smith pressed the broad face of the ax hard and heavily on the stone, which made the turning of it very fatiguing. The man came every now and then from the wheel to see how the work went on, and at length would take his ax as it was, without further grinding. "No," said the smith, "turn on, turn on; we shall have it bright by-and-by; as yet, it is only speckled." "Yes," said the man, "but *I think I like a speckled ax best*."

And I believe this may have been the case with many, who, having, for want of some such means as I employed, found the difficulty of obtaining good and breaking bad habits in other points of vice and virtue, have given up the struggle, and concluded that "*a speckled ax is best*"; for something, that pretended to be reason, was every now and then suggesting to me that such extreme nicety as I exacted of myself might be a kind of foppery in morals, which, if it were known, would make me ridiculous; that a perfect character might be attended with the inconvenience of being envied and hated; and that a benevolent man should allow a few faults in himself, to keep his friends in countenance.

In truth, I found myself incorrigible with respect to *Order*; and now I am grown old, and my memory bad, I feel very sensibly the want of it. But, on the whole, though I never arrived at the perfection I had been so ambitious of obtaining, but fell far short of it, yet I was, by the endeavor, a better and a happier man than I otherwise should have been if I had not attempted it; as those who aim at perfect writing by imitating the engraved copies, though they never reach the wished-for excellence of those copies, their hand is mended by the endeavor, and is tolerable while it continues fair and legible.

It may be well my posterity should be informed that to this little artifice, with the blessing of God, their ancestor owed the constant felicity of his life, down to his seventy-ninth year, in which this is written. What reverses may attend the remainder is in the hand of Providence; but, if they arrive, the reflection on past happiness enjoyed ought to help his bearing them with more resignation.

To *Temperance* he ascribes his long-continued health, and what is still left to him of a good constitution; to *Industry and Frugality*, the early easiness of his circumstances and acquisition of his fortune, with all that knowledge that enabled him to be a useful citizen, and obtained for him some degree of reputation among the learned; to *Sincerity* and *Justice*, the confidence of his country, and the honorable employs it conferred upon him; and to the joint influence of the whole mass of the virtues, even in the imperfect state he was able to acquire them, all that evenness of temper, and that cheerfulness in conversation, which makes his company still sought for, and agreeable even to his young acquaintance. I hope, therefore, that some of my descendants may follow the example and reap the benefit.

It will be remarked that, though my scheme was not wholly without religion, there was in it no mark of any of the distinguishing tenets of any particular sect. I had purposely avoided them; for, being fully persuaded of the utility and excellency of my method, and that it might be serviceable to people in all religions, and intending some time or other to publish it, I would-not have any thing in it that should prejudice any one, of any sect, against it. I proposed writing a little comment on each virtue, in which I would have shown the advantages of possessing it, and the mischiefs attending its opposite vice; I should have called my book THE ART OF VIRTUE, because it would have shown the means and manner of obtaining virtue, which would have distinguished it from the mere exhortation to be good, that does not instruct and indicate the means, but is like the apostle's man of verbal charity, who, without showing to the naked and hungry how or where they might get clothes or victuals, only exhorted them to be fed and clothed. —*James, ii., 15, 16.*

But it so happened that my intention of writing and publishing this comment was never fulfilled. I had, indeed, from time to time, put down short hints of the sentiments and reasoning to be made use of in it, some of which I have still by me; but the necessary close attention to private business in the earlier part of life, and public business since, have occasioned my postponing it; for, it being connected in my mind with *a great and extensive project,* that required the whole man to execute, and which an unforeseen succession of employs prevented my attending to, it has hitherto remained unfinished.

In this piece it was my design to explain and enforce this doctrine, *that vicious actions are not hurtful because they are forbidden, but forbidden because they are hurtful,* the nature of man alone considered; that it was, therefore, every one's interest to be virtuous who wished to be happy even in this world; and I should, from this circumstance (there being always in the world a number of rich merchants, nobility, states, and princes, who have need of honest instruments for the management of their affairs, and such being so rare), have endeavored to convince young persons that no qualities are so likely to make a poor man's fortune as those of *probity* and *integrity.*

My list of virtues contained at first but twelve; but a Quaker friend having kindly informed me that I was generally thought proud; that my pride showed itself frequently in conversation; that I was not content with being in the right when discussing any point, but was overbearing, and rather insolent, of which he convinced me by mentioning several instances; I determined to endeavor to cure myself, if I could, of this vice or folly among the rest, and I added *Humility* to my list, giving an extensive meaning to the word.

I can not boast of much success in acquiring the *reality* of this virtue, but I had a good deal with regard to the appearance of it. I made it a rule to forbear all direct contradiction to the sentiments of others, and all positive assertion of my own. I even forbid myself the use of every word or expression in the language that imported a fixed opinion, such as *certainly*, *undoubtedly*, *&c.*, and I adopted, instead of them, *I conceive*, *I apprehend*, or *I imagine* a thing to be so or so; or *it so appears to me at present.* When another asserted something that I thought an error, I denied myself the pleasure of contradicting him abruptly, and of showing immediately some absurdity in his proposition; and in answering I began by observing that in certain cases or circumstances his opinion would be right, but in the present case there *appeared* or *seemed to me* some difference, &c. I soon found the advantage of this change in my manners; the conversations I engaged in went on more pleasantly. The modest way in which I proposed my opinions procured them a readier reception and less contradiction; I had less mortification when I was found to be in the wrong, and I more easily prevailed with others to give up their mistakes and join with me when I happened to be in the right.

And this mode, which I at first put on with some violence to natural inclination, became at length easy, and so habitual to me, that perhaps for the last fifty years no one has ever heard a dogmatical expression escape me. And to this habit (after my character of integrity) I think it principally owing that I had early so much weight with my fellow-citizens when I proposed new institutions, or alterations in the old, and so much influence in public councils when I became a member; for I was but a bad speaker, never eloquent, subject to much hesitation in my choice of words, hardly correct in language, and yet I generally carried my point.

In reality, there is, perhaps, no one of our natural passions so hard to subdue as *pride*. Disguise it, struggle with it, stifle it, mortify it as much as one pleases, it is still alive, and will every now and then peep out and show itself; you will see it, perhaps, often in this history; for, even if I could conceive that I had completely overcome it, I should probably be *proud* of my *humility*.

❧

I Can

Ralph Waldo Emerson
(1803–1882)

So NIGH is grandeur to our dust,
So near is God to man,
When Duty whispers low, Thou must,
The youth replies, I can.

❧

Look on the Sunny Side

Helen Steiner Rice
(1901–1981)

THERE ARE always two sides,
    the GOOD and the BAD,
The DARK and the LIGHT,
    the SAD and the GLAD—
But in looking back over
    the GOOD and the BAD
We're aware of the number
    of GOOD THINGS we've had—
And in counting our blessings
    we find when we're through
We've no reason at all
    to complain or be blue—
So thank God for GOOD things
    He has already done;
And be grateful to Him
    for the battles you've won,
And know that the same God
    who helped you before

Is ready and willing
    to help you once more—
Then with faith in your heart
    reach out for God's Hand
And accept what He sends,
    though you can't understand—
For OUR FATHER in heaven
    always knows what is best,
And if you trust in His wisdom
    your life will be blest,
For always remember
    that whatever betides you,
You are never alone
    for God is beside you.

EDITOR WILLIAM ALLEN WHITE wrote a moving editorial for the *Emporia Gazette* about Mary White, his daughter, who had died. I find the grief, love, and pride of the famous editor most affecting.

47

Mary White

William Allen White
(1868–1944)

THE ASSOCIATED PRESS reports carrying the news of Mary White's death declared that it came as a result of a fall from a horse. How she would have hooted at that! She never fell from a horse in her life. Horses have fallen on her and with her—"I'm always trying to hold 'em in my lap," she used to say. But she was proud of few things, and one was that she could ride anything that had four legs and hair. Her death resulted not from a fall, but from a blow on the head which fractured her skull, and the blow came from the limb of an overhanging tree on the parking.

The last hour of her life was typical of its happiness. She came home from a day's work at school, topped off by a hard grind with the copy on the High School Annual, and felt that a ride would refresh her. She climbed into her khakis, chattering to her mother about the work she was doing, and hurried to get her horse and be put out on the dirt roads for the country air and the radiant green fields of the spring. As she rode through the town on an easy gallop, she kept waving at passers-by. She knew everyone in town. For a decade the little figure with the long pig-tail and the red hair-ribbon has been familiar on the streets of Emporia, and she got in the way of speaking to those who nodded at her. She passed the Kerrs—walking the horse—in front of the Normal Library, and waved at them; passed another friend a few hundred feet further on, and waved at her. The horse was walking and, as she turned into North Merchant Street, she took off her cowboy hat, and the horse swung into a lope. She passed the Tripletts and waved her cowboy hat at them, still moving gayly north on Merchant Street. A *Gazette* carrier passed—a High School boy friend—and she waved at him, but with her bridle hand; the horse veered quickly, plunged into the parking where the low-hanging limb faced her, and, while she still looked back waving, the blow came. But she did not fall from the horse; she slipped off, dazed a bit, staggered, and fell in a faint. She never quite recovered consciousness.

But she did not fall from the horse, neither was she riding fast. A year or so ago she used to go like the wind. But that habit was broken, and she used the horse to get into the open to get fresh, hard exercise and to work off a certain surplus energy that welled up in her and needed a physical out-let. That need has been in her heart for years. It was back of the impulse that kept the dauntless little brown-clad figure on the streets and country roads of this community and built into a strong, muscular body what had been a frail and sickly frame during the first years of her life. But the riding gave her more than a body. It released a gay and hardy soul. She was the happiest thing in the world. And she was happy because she was enlarging her horizon. She came to know all sorts and conditions of men; Charley O'Brien, the traffic cop, was one of her best friends. W. L. Holtz, the Latin teacher, was another. Tom O'Connor, farmer-politician, and Rev. J. H. J. Rice, preacher and police judge, and Frank Beach, music master, were her special friends, and all the girls, black and white, above the track and below the track, in Pepville and Stringtown, were among her acquaintances. And she brought home riotous stories of her adventures. She loved to rollick;

persiflage was her natural expression at home. Her humor was a continual bubble of joy. She seemed to think in hyperbole and metaphor. She was mischievous without malice, as full of faults as an old shoe. No angel was Mary White, but an easy girl to live with, for she never nursed a grouch five minutes in her life.

With all her eagerness for the out-of-doors, she loved books. On her table when she left her room were a book by Conrad, one by Galsworthy, *Creative Chemistry*, by E. E. Slosson, and a Kipling book. She read Mark Twain, Dickens, and Kipling before she was ten—all of their writings. Wells and Arnold Bennett particularly amused and diverted her. She was entered as a student in Wellesley in 1922; was assistant editor of the High School Annual this year, and in line for election to the editorship of the Annual next year. She was a member of the executive committee of the High School Y.W.C.A.

Within the last two years she had begun to be moved by an ambition to draw. She began as most children do by scribbling in her school books, funny pictures. She bought cartoon magazines and took a course—rather casually, naturally, for she was, after all, a child with no strong purposes— and this year she tasted the first fruits of success by having her pictures accepted by the High School Annual. But the thrill of delight she got when Mr. Ecord, of the Normal Annual, asked her to do the cartooning for that book this spring was too beautiful for words. She fell to her work with all her enthusiastic heart. Her drawings were accepted, and her pride—always repressed by a lively sense of the ridiculousness of the figure she was cutting—was a really gorgeous thing to see. No successful artist ever drank a deeper draft of satisfaction than she took from the little fame her work was getting among her schoolfellows. In her glory she almost forgot her horse—but never her car.

For she used the car as a jitney bus. It was her social life. She never had a "party" in all her nearly seventeen years—wouldn't have one; but she never drove a block in the car in her life that she didn't begin to fill the car with pick-ups! Everyone rode with Mary White—white and black, old and young, rich and poor, men and women. She liked nothing better than to fill the car full of long-legged High School boys and an occasional girl, and parade the town. She never had a "date," nor went to a dance, except once with her brother Bill, and the "boy proposition" didn't interest her—yet. But young people—great spring-breaking, vanish-cracking, fender-bending, door-sagging carloads of "kids"—gave her great pleasure. Her zests were keen. But the most fun she ever had in her life was acting as chairman of the committee that got up the big turkey dinner for the poor folks at the county home; scores of pies, gallons of slaw, jam, cakes, preserves, oranges, and a wilderness of turkey were loaded in the car and taken to the county home. And, being of a practical turn of mind, she risked her own Christmas dinner by staying to see that the poor folks actually got it all. Not that she was a cynic; she just disliked to tempt folks. While there she found a blind colored uncle, very old, who could do nothing but make rag rugs, and she rustled up from her school friends rags enough to keep him busy for a season. The last engagement she tried to make was to take the guests at the county home out for a car ride. And the last endeavor of her life was to try to get a rest room for colored girls in the High School. She found one girl reading in the toilet, because there was no better place for a colored girl to loaf, and it inflamed her sense of injustice and she became a nagging harpie to those who, she thought, could remedy the evil. The poor she had always with her, and was glad of it. She hungered and thirsted for righteousness; and was the most impious creature in the world. She joined the Congregational Church without consulting her parents; not particularly for her soul's good. She never had a thrill of piety in her life, and would have hooted at "testimony." But even as a little child she felt the church was an agency for helping people to more of life's abundance, and she wanted to help. She never wanted help for herself. Clothes meant little to her. It was a fight to get a new rig on her; but eventually a harder fight to get it off. She never wore a jewel and had no ring but her High School class ring, and never asked for anything but a wrist watch. She refused to have her hair up, though she was nearly seventeen. "Mother," she protested, "you don't know how much I get by with, in my braided pig-tails, that I could not with my hair up." Above every other passion of her life was her passion not to grow up, to be a child. The tomboy in her, which was big, seemed to loathe to be put away forever in skirts. She was a Peter Pan, who refused to grow up.

Her funeral yesterday at the Congregational Church was as she would have wished it; no singing, no flowers save the big bunch of red roses from her Brother Bill's Harvard classmen—Heavens, how proud that would have made her!—and the red roses from the *Gazette* force—in vases at her head and feet. A short prayer, Paul's beautiful essay on "Love" from the Thirteenth Chapter of First Corinthians, some remarks about her democratic spirit by her friend, John H. J. Rice, pastor and police judge, which she would have deprecated if she could, a prayer sent down for her by her friend, Carl Nau, and opening the service the slow, poignant movement from Beethoven's *Moonlight Sonata*, which she loved, and closing the service a cutting from the joyously melancholy first movement of Tschaikowski's *Pathetic Symphony*, which she liked to hear in certain moods on the phonograph, then the Lord's Prayer by her friends in the High School.

That was all.

For her pall-bearers only her friends were chosen: her Latin teacher, W. L. Holtz, her High School principal, Rice Brown, her doctor, Frank Foncannon; her friend, W. W. Finney; her pal at the *Gazette* office, Walter Hughes; and her brother Bill. It would have made her smile to know that her friend Charley O'Brien, the traffic cop, had been transferred from Sixth and Commercial to the corner near the church to direct her friends who came to bid her good-by.

A rift in the clouds in a gray day threw a shaft of sunlight upon her coffin as her nervous energetic little body sank to its last sleep. But the soul of her, the glowing, gorgeous, fervent soul of her, surely was flaming in eager joy upon some other dawn.

Little Boy Blue

Eugene Field
(1850–1895)

THE LITTLE TOY DOG is covered with dust,
    But sturdy and stanch he stands;
And the little toy soldier is red with rust,
    And his musket moulds in his hands.
Time was when the little toy dog was new,
    And the soldier was passing fair,
And that was the time when our Little Boy Blue
    Kissed them and put them there.

"Now, don't you go till I come," he said,
    "And don't you make any noise!"
So toddling off to his trundle-bed
    He dreamt of the pretty toys.
And as he was dreaming, an angel song
    Awakened our Little Boy Blue,—
Oh, the years are many, the years are long,
    But the little toy friends are true!

Ay, faithful to Little Boy Blue they stand,
    Each in the same old place,
Awaiting the touch of a little hand,
    The smile of a little face.
And they wonder, as waiting these long years through,
    In the dust of that little chair,
What has become of our Little Boy Blue
    Since he kissed them and put them there.

❧

The Eternal Goodness

John Greenleaf Whittier
(1807–1892)

I SEE the wrong that round me lies,
    I feel the guilt within;
I hear, with groan and travail-cries,
    The world confess its sin.

Yet, in the maddening maze of things,
    And tossed by storm and flood,
To one fixed trust my spirit clings:
    I know that God is good!

❧

ELBERT HUBBARD WAS an American lecturer and essayist. He was also a successful magazine publisher. "A Message to Garcia" (1899) was a thrilling account of an army officer's ability to get things done, however difficult. This is a lesson on: "It must be done and I can do it."

A Message to Garcia
Elbert Hubbard
(1865–1915)

IN ALL THIS Cuban business there is one man stands out on the horizon of my memory.

When war broke out between Spain and the United States, it was very necessary to communicate quickly with the leader of the Insurgents. Garcia was somewhere in the mountain fastnesses of Cuba—no one knew where. No mail or telegraph message could reach him. The President must secure his cooperation, and quickly.

What to do!

Someone said to the President, "There is a fellow by the name of Rowan will find Garcia for you, if anybody can."

Rowan was sent for and given a letter to be delivered to Garcia. How the "fellow by the name of Rowan" took the letter, sealed it up in an oilskin pouch, strapped it over his heart, in four days landed by night off the coast of Cuba from an open boat, disappeared into the jungle, and in three weeks came out on the other side of the Island, having traversed a hostile country on foot, and delivered his letter to Garcia—are things I have no special de-

sire to tell in detail. The point that I wish to make is this: McKinley gave Rowan a letter to be delivered to Garcia; Rowan took the letter and did not ask, "Where is he at?"

By the Eternal! there is a man whose form should be cast in deathless bronze and the statue placed in every college of the land. It is not book-learning young men need, nor instruction about this and that, but a stiff-ening of the vertebrae which will cause them to be loyal to a trust, to act promptly, concentrate their energies: do the thing—"Carry a message to Garcia."

General Garcia is dead now, but there are other Garcias. No man who has endeavored to carry out an enterprise where many hands were needed, but has been well-nigh appalled at times by the imbecility of the average man—the inability or unwillingness to concentrate on a thing and do it.

Slipshod assistance, foolish inattention, dowdy indifference, and half-hearted work seem the rule; and no man succeeds, unless by hook or crook or threat he forces or bribes other men to assist him; or mayhap, God in His goodness performs a miracle, and sends him an Angel of Light for an assistant.

You, reader, put this matter to a test: You are sitting now in your of-fice—six clerks are within call. Summon any one and make this request: "Please look in the encyclopedia and make a brief memorandum for me concerning the life of Correggio."

Will the clerk quietly say, "Yes, sir," and go do the task?

On your life he will not. He will look at you out of a fishy eye and ask one or more of the following questions:

Who was he?

Which encyclopedia?

Where is the encyclopedia?

Was I hired for that?

Don't you mean Bismarck?

What's the matter with Charlie doing it?

Is he dead?

Is there any hurry?

Sha'n't I bring you the book and let you look it up yourself?

What do you want to know for?

And I will lay you ten to one that after you have answered the questions, and explained how to find the information, and why you want it, the clerk will go off and get one of the other clerks to help him try to find Garcia—and then come back and tell you there is no such man. Of course I may lose my bet, but according to the Law of Average I will not.

Now, if you are wise, you will not bother to explain to your "assistant" that Correggio is indexed under the C's, not in the K's, but you will smile very sweetly and say, "Never mind," and go look it up yourself. And this incapacity for independent action, this moral stupidity, this infirmity of the will, this unwillingness to cheerfully catch hold and lift . . . If men will not act for themselves, what will they do when the benefit of their effort is for all?

A first mate with knotted club seems necessary; and the dread of getting "the bounce" Saturday night holds many a worker to his place.

Advertise for a stenographer, and nine out of ten who apply can neither spell nor punctuate—and do not think it necessary to.

Can such a one write a letter to Garcia?

"You see that bookkeeper," said the foreman to me in a large factory.

"Yes; what about him?"

"Well, he's a fine accountant, but if I'd send him up town on an errand, he might accomplish the errand all right, and on the other hand, might stop at four saloons on the way, and when he got to Main Street would forget what he had been sent for."

Can such a man be entrusted to carry a message to Garcia?

We have recently been hearing much maudlin sympathy expressed for the "downtrodden denizens of the sweatshop" and the "homeless wanderer searching for honest employment," and with it all often go many hard words for the men in power.

Nothing is said about the employer who grows old before his time in a vain attempt to get frowsy ne'er-do-wells to do intelligent work; and his long, patient striving after "help" that does nothing but loaf when his back is turned. In every store and factory there is a constant weeding out process going on. The employer is constantly sending away "help" that have shown their incapacity to further the interests of the business, and others are being taken on. No matter how good times are, this sorting continues: only, if times are hard and work is scarce, the sorting is done finer—but out and forever out the incompetent and unworthy go. It is the survival of the fittest. Self-interest prompts every employer to keep the best—those who can carry a message to Garcia.

I know one man of really brilliant parts who has not the ability to manage a business of his own, and yet who is absolutely worthless to anyone else, because he carries with him constantly the insane suspicion that his employer is oppressing, or intending to oppress, him. He cannot give orders, and he will not receive them. Should a message be given him to take to Garcia, his answer would probably be, "Take it yourself!"

Tonight this man walks the streets looking for work, the wind whistling through his threadbare coat. No one who knows him dare employ him, for he is a regular firebrand of discontent. He is impervious to reason, and the only thing that can impress him is the toe of a thick-soled Number Nine boot.

Of course, I know that one so morally deformed is no less to be pitied than a physical cripple; but in our pitying let us drop a tear, too, for the men who are striving to carry on a great enterprise, whose working hours are not limited by the whistle, and whose hair is fast turning white through the struggle to hold in line dowdy indifference, slipshod imbecility, and the heartless ingratitude which, for their enterprise, would be both hungry and homeless.

Have I put the matter too strongly? Possibly I have; but when all the world has gone aslumming I wish to speak a word of sympathy for the man who succeeds—the man who, against great odds, has directed the efforts of others, and having succeeded, finds there's nothing in it: nothing but bare board and clothes. I have carried a dinner-pail and worked for day's wages, and I have also been an employer of labor, and I know there is something to be said on both sides. There is no excellence, per se, in poverty; rags are no

recommendation; and all employers are not rapacious and high-handed, any more than all poor men are virtuous. My heart goes out to the man who does his work when the "boss" is away, as well as when he is at home. And the man who, when given a letter for Garcia, quietly takes the missive, without asking any idiotic questions, and with no lurking intention of chucking it into the nearest sewer, or of doing aught else but deliver it, never gets "laid off," nor has to go on a strike for higher wages. Civilization is one long, anxious search for just such individuals. Anything such a man asks shall be granted. He is wanted in every city, town and village—in every office, shop, store and factory. The world cries out for such; he is needed and needed badly—the man who can "Carry a Message to Garcia."

❦

Not in Vain

Emily Dickinson
(1830–1886)

IF I CAN STOP one heart from breaking,
I shall not live in vain:
If I can ease one life the aching,
Or cool one pain,
Or help one fainting robin
Unto his nest again,
I shall not live in vain.

Be Strong

Maltbie Davenport Babcock
(1858–1901)

BE STRONG!
We are not here to play, to dream, to drift;
We have hard work to do, and loads to lift;
Shun not the struggle—face it; 'tis God's gift.

Be strong!
Say not, "The days are evil. Who's to blame?"
And fold the hands and acquiesce—oh shame!
Stand up, speak out, and bravely, in God's name.

Be strong!
It matters not how deep intrenched the wrong,
How hard the battle goes, the day how long;
Faint not—fight on! To-morrow comes the song.

WHEN I WAS a young man I went one Sunday morning to give a talk in the chapel of an old and famous New England university. The chapel was filled with students and faculty.

I was startled at the close of my address because the students began a great snapping of fingers. Afterward, an elderly professor took me to his home for lunch, and I asked, "Why the general snapping of fingers at the close of my talk?"

"Oh, that is their form of applause in chapel in lieu of handclapping," he explained.

As I prepared to leave, my host presented me with a little book, *Courage* by J. M. Barrie. "You are young and have a long life ahead and you will need courage all along the way," he said. "This will help you." It has helped. I have it still. It was Barrie's 1922 rectorial address at St. Andrews University in Scotland.

The speech is so wise and expressed in such gracious words that I include it here almost whole. It is one of the world's greatest masterpieces of spoken English.

Courage

J. M. Barrie (1860–1957)

YOU HAVE HAD many rectors here in St. Andrews who will continue in bloom long after the lowly ones such as I am are dead and rotten and forgotten. They are the roses in December; you remember some one said that God gave us memory so that we might have roses in December. But I do not envy the great ones. In my experience—and you may find in the end it

is yours also—the people I have cared for—my December roses—have been very simple folk. Yet I wish that for this hour I could swell into someone of importance, so as I do you credit. I suppose you had a melting for me because I was hewn out of one of your own quarries, walked similar academic groves, and have trudged the road on which you will soon set forth. I would that I could put into your hands a staff for that somewhat bloody march, for though there is much about myself that I conceal from other people, to help you I would expose every cranny of my mind.

But, alas, when the hour strikes for the Rector to answer to his call he is unable to become the undergraduate he used to be, and so the only door into you is closed. We, your elders, are much more interested in you than you are in us. We are not really important to you. I have utterly forgotten the address of the Rector of my time, and even who he was, but I recall vividly climbing up a statue to tie his colours around its neck and being hurled therefrom the contumely. We remember the important things. I cannot provide you with that staff for your journey; but perhaps I can tell you a little about it, how to use it and lose it and find it again, and cling to it more than ever. You shall cut it—so it is ordained—every one of you for himself, and its name is Courage. You must excuse me if I talk a good deal about courage to you to-day. There is nothing else much worth speaking about to undergraduates or graduates or white-haired men and women. It is the lovely virtue—the rib of Himself that God sent down to His children.

My special difficulty is that though you have had literary rectors here before, they were the big guns, the historians, the philosophers; you have

had none, I think, who followed my more humble branch, which may be described as playing hide and seek with angels. My puppets seem more real to me than myself, and I could get on much more swingingly if I made one of them deliver this address. It is M'Connachie who has brought me to this pass. M'Connachie, I should explain, as I have undertaken to open the innermost doors, is the name I give to the unruly half of myself: the writing half. We are complement and supplement. I am the half that is dour and practical and canny, he is the fanciful half; my desire is to be the family solicitor, standing firm on my hearthrug among the harsh realities of the office furniture; while he prefers to fly around on one wing. I should not mind him doing that, but he drags me with him. I have sworn that M'Connachie shall not interfere with the address today; but there is no telling. I might have done things worthwhile if it had not been for M'Connachie, and my first piece of advice to you at any rate shall be sound: don't copy me. A good subject for a rectorial address would be the mess the Rector himself has made of life. I merely cast this forth as a suggestion, and leave the working of it out to my successor. I do not think it has been used yet.

My theme is Courage, as you should use it in the great fight that seems to be coming between youth and their betters; by youth, meaning, of course, you, and by your betters, us. I want you to take up this position: That youth have for too long left exclusively in our hands the decisions in national matters that are more vital to them than to us. Things about the next war, for instance, and why the last one ever had a beginning. I use the word fight because it must, I think, begin with a challenge; but the aim is

the reverse of antagonism, it is partnership. I want you to hold that the time has arrived for youth to demand that partnership, and to demand it courageously. That to gain courage is what you come to St. Andrews for, with some alarums and excursions into college life. That is what I propose, but, of course, the issue lies with M'Connachie.

Your betters had no share in the immediate cause of the war; we know what nation has that blot to wipe out; but for fifty years or so we heeded not the rumblings of the distant drum—I do not mean by lack of military preparations; and when war did come we told youth, who had to get us out of it, tall tales of what it really is and of the clover beds to which it leads. We were not meaning to deceive, most of us were as honourable and as ignorant as the youth themselves; but that does not acquit us of failings such as stupidity and jealousy, the two black spots in human nature which, more than love of money, are at the root of all evil. If you prefer to leave things as they are we shall probably fail you again. Do not be too sure that we have learned our lesson, and are not at this very moment doddering down some brimstone path.

I am far from implying that even worse things than war may not come to a State. There are circumstances in which nothing can so well become a land, as I think this land proved which the late war did break out and there was but one thing to do. There is a form of anaemia that is more rotting than even an unjust war. The end will indeed have come to our courage and to us when we are afraid in dire mischance to refer the final appeal to the arbitrament of arms. I suppose all the lusty of our race alive and dead, join hands on that.

And he is dead who will not fight;
And who dies fighting has increase.

But if you must be in the struggle, the more reason you should know why, before it begins and have a say in the decision whether, it is to begin. The youth who went to the war had no such knowledge, no such say; I am sure the survivors, of whom there must be a number here today, want you to be wiser that they were, and are certainly determined to be wiser next time themselves. If you are to get that partnership which, once gained, is to be for, mutual benefit it will be, I should say, by banding yourselves, with these men, not defiantly but firmly, not for selfish ends but for your country's good. In the meantime they have one bulwark; they have a General who is befriending them as I think never, after the fighting was over, has a General befriended his men before. Perhaps the seemly thing would be for us, their betters, to elect one of these young survivors of the carnage to be our Rector. He ought now to know a few things about war that are worth our hearing. If his theme were the Rector's favourite, diligence, I should be afraid of his advising a great many of us to be diligent in sitting still and doing no more harm.

Of course he would put it more suavely than that, though it is not, I think, by gentleness that you will get your rights; we are dogged ones at sticking to what we have got, and so will you be at our age. But avoid calling us ugly names; we may be stubborn and we may be blunderers, but we love you more than aught else in the world, and once you have won your partnership we shall all be welcoming you. I urge you not to use ugly names

about any one. In the war it was not the fighting men who were distinguished for abuse; as has been well said, "Hell hath no fury like a non-combatant." Never ascribe to an opponent motives meaner than your own. There may be students here to-day who have decided this session to go in for immortality, and would like to know of an easy way of accomplishing it. That is a way, but not so easy as you think. Go through life without ever ascribing to your opponents motives meaner than your own. Nothing so lowers the moral currency; give it up, and be great.

Another sure way to fame is to know what you mean. It is a solemn thought that almost no one—if he is truly eminent—knows what he means. Look at the great ones of the earth, the politicians. We do not discuss what they say but what they may, have meant when they said it. In 1922 we are all wondering, and so are they, what they meant in 1914 and afterwards. They are publishing books trying to find out; the men of action as well as the men of words. There are exceptions. It is not that our statesmen are "sugared mouths with minds therefrae"; many of them are the best men we have got, upright and anxious, nothing cheaper than to miscall them. The explanation seems just to be that it is so difficult to know what you mean, especially when you have become a swell. No longer, apparently, can you deal in "russet yeas and honest kersey noes"; gone for ever is simplicity, which is as beautiful as the divine plain face of Lamb's Miss Kelly. Doubts breed suspicions, a dangerous air. Without suspicion there might have been no war. When you are called to Downing Street to discuss what you want of your betters with the Prime Minister, he won't be suspicious, not as far as you can see; but remember the atmosphere or generations you

are in, and when he passes you the toast-rack say to yourselves, if you would be in the mode, "Now, I wonder what he meant by that."

Even without striking out in the way I suggest, you are already disturbing your betters considerably. I sometimes talk this over with M'Connachie, with whom, as you may guess, circumstances compel me to pass a good deal of my time. In our talks we agree that we, your betters, constantly find you forgetting that we are your betters. Your answer is that the war and other happenings have shown you that age is not necessarily another name for sapience; that our avoidance of frankness in life and in the arts is often, but not so often as you think, a cowardly way of shirking unpalatable truths, and that you have taken us off our pedestals because we look more natural on the ground. You who are at the rash age even accuse your elders, sometimes not without justification, of being more rash than yourselves. "If Youth but only knew," we used to teach you to sing; but now, just because Youth has been to the war, it wants to change the next line into "If Age had only to do."

In so far as this attitude of yours is merely passive, sullen, negative, as it mainly is, despairing of our capacity and anticipating a future of gloom, it is no game for man or woman. It is certainly the opposite of that for which I plead. Do not stand aloof, despising, disbelieving, but come in and help insist on coming in and helping. After all, we have shown a good deal of courage; and your part is to add a greater courage to it. There are glorious years lying ahead of you if you choose to make them glorious. God's in His heaven still. So forward, brave hearts. To what adventures I cannot tell, but I know that your God is watching to see whether you are adventurous. I know that the great partnership is only a first step, but I do not know what are to be the next and the next. The partnership is but a tool; what are you to do with it? Very little, I warn you, if you are merely thinking of yourselves; much, if what is at the marrow of your thoughts is a future that even you can scarcely hope to see.

Learn as a beginning how world-shaking situations arise and how they may be countered. Doubt all your betters who would deny you that right of partnership. Begin by doubting all such in high places except, of course, your professors. But doubt all other professors—yet not conceitedly, as some do, with their noses in the air; avoid all such physical risks. If it necessitates your pushing some of us out of our places, still push; you will find it needs some shoving. But the things courage can do! The things that even incompetence can do if it works with singleness of purpose. The war has done at least one big thing: it has taken spring out of the year. And, this accomplished, our leading people are amazed to find that the other seasons are not conducting themselves as usual. The spring of the year lies buried in the fields of France and elsewhere. By the time the next eruption comes it may be you who are responsible for it and your sons who are in the lava. All, perhaps, because this year you let things slide.

We are a nice and kindly people, but it is already evident that we are stealing back into the old grooves, seeking cushions for our old bones, rather than attempting to build up a fairer future. That is what we mean when we say that the country is settling down. Make haste, or you will become like us, with only the thing we proudly call experience to add to your stock, a poor exchange for the generous feelings that time will take away.

We have no intention of giving you your share. Look around and see how much share Youth has now that the war is over. You got a handsome share while it lasted.

I expect we shall beat you; unless your fortitude be doubly girded by a desire to send a message of cheer to your brothers who fell, the only message, I believe, for which they crave; they are not worrying about their Aunt Jane. They want to know if you have learned wisely from what befell them; if you have, they will be braced in the feeling that they did not die in vain. Some of them think they did. They will not take our word for it that they did not. You are their living image; they know you could not lie to them, but they distrust our flattery and our cunning faces. To us they have passed away; but are you who stepped into their heritage only yesterday, whose books are scarcely cold to their hands, you who still hear their cries being blown across the links are you already relegating them to the shades? The gaps they have left in this University are among the most honourable of her wounds. But we are not here to acclaim them. Where they are now, hero is, I think, a very little word. They call to you to find out in time the truth about this great game, which your elders play for stakes and Youth plays for its life.

I do not know whether you are grown a little tired of that word hero, but I am sure the heroes are. That is the subject of one of our unfinished plays, M'Connachie is the one who writes the plays. If any one of you here proposes to be playwright you can take this for your own and finish it. The scene is a school, schoolmasters present, but if you like you could make it a university, professors present. They are discussing an illuminated scroll

71

about a student fallen in the war, which they have kindly presented to his parents; and unexpectedly the parents enter. They are an old pair, back-bent, they have been stalwarts in their day but have now gone small; they are poor, but not so poor that they could not send their boy to college. They are in black, not such a rusty black either, and you may be sure she is the one who knows what to do with his hat. Their faces are gnarled, I sup-pose—but I do not need to describe that pair to Scottish students. They have come to thank the Senatus for their lovely scroll and to ask them to tear it up. At first they had been enamoured to read of what a scholar their son was, how noble and adored by all. But soon a fog settled over them, for this grand person was not the boy they knew. He had many a fault well known to them; he was not always so noble; as a scholar he did no more than scrape through; and he sometimes made his father rage and his mother grieve. They had liked to talk such memories as these together, and smile over them, as if they were bits of him he had left lying about the house. So thank you kindly, and would you please give them back their boy by tearing up the scroll? I see nothing else for our dramatist to do. I think he should ask an alumna of St. Andrews to play the old lady (indicating Miss Ellen Terry). The loveliest of all young actresses, the dearest of all old ones; it seems only yesterday that all the men of imagination proposed to their beloved in some such frenzied words as these, "As I can't get Miss Terry, may I have you?"

This play might become historical as the opening of your propaganda in the proposed campaign. How to make a practical advance? The League of Nations is a very fine thing, but it cannot save you, because it will be run by us. Beware your betters bringing presents. What is wanted is something run by yourselves. You have more in common with the youth of other lands than Youth and Age can ever have with each other; even the hostile countries sent out many a son very like ours, from the same sort of homes, the same sort of universities, who had as little to do as our youth had with the origin of the great adventure. Can we doubt that many of these on both sides who have gone over and were once opponents are now friends? You ought to have a League of Youth of all countries as your beginning, ready to say to all Governments, "We will fight each other, but only when we are sure of the necessity." Are you equal to your job, you young men? If not, I call upon the red-gowned women to lead the way. I sound to myself as if I were advocating a rebellion, though I am really asking for a larger friendship. Perhaps I may be arrested on leaving the hall. In such a cause I should think that I had at last proved myself worthy to be your Rector.

You will have to work harder than ever, but possibly not so much at the same things; more at modern languages certainly if you are to discuss that League of Youth with the students of other nations when they come over to St. Andrews for the Conference. I am far from taking a side against the classics. I should as soon argue against your having tops to your heads; that way lie the best tops. Science, too, has at last come to its own in St. Andrews. It is the surest means of teaching you how to know what you mean when you say. So you will have to work harder. Izaak Walton quotes the saying that doubtless the Almighty could have created a finer fruit than the strawberry, but that doubtless also He never did. Doubtless also He could have provided us with better fun than hard work, but I don't know what it is. To be born poor is probably the next best thing. The greatest glory that has ever come to me was to be swallowed up in London, not knowing a soul, with no means of subsistence, and the fun of working till the stars went out. To have known any one would have spoilt it. I did not even quite know the language. I rang for my boots, and they thought I said a glass of water, so I drank the water and worked on. There was no food in the cupboard, so I did not need to waste time in eating. The pangs and agonies when no proof came. How courteously tolerant was I of the postman without a proof for us; how M'Connachie, on the other hand, wanted to punch his head. The magic days when our article appeared in an evening paper. The promptitude with which I counted the lines to see how much we should get for it. Then M'Connachie's superb air of dropping it into the gutter. Oh, to be a free lance of journalism again—that darling jade! Those were days. Too good to last. Let us be grave. Here comes a Rector.

But now, on reflection, a dreadful sinking assails me, that this was not really work. The artistic callings—you remember how Stevenson thumped them—are merely doing what you are clamorous to be at; it is not real work unless you would rather be doing something else. My so-called labours were just M'Connachie running away with me. Still, I have sometimes worked; for instance, I feel that I am working at this moment. And the big guns are in the same plight as the little ones. Carlyle, the king of all rectors, has always been accepted as the arch-apostle of toil, and has registered his many woes. But it will not do. Despite sickness, poortith, want and all, he was grinding all his life at the one job he revelled in. An extraordinarily happy man, though there is no direct proof that he thought so.

There must be many men in other callings besides the arts lauded as hard workers who are merely out for enjoyment. Our Chancellor? (indicating Lord Haig). If our Chancellor had always a passion to be a soldier, we must reconsider him as a worker. Even our Principal? How about the light that burns in our Principal's room after decent people have gone to bed? If we could climb up and look in—I should like to do something of that kind for the last time—should we find him engaged in honest toil, or guiltily engrossed in chemistry?

You will all fall into one of those two callings, the joyous or the uncongenial; and one wishes you into the first, though our sympathy, our esteem, must go rather to the less fortunate, the braver ones who "turn their necessity to glorious gain" after they have put away their dreams. To the others will go the easy prizes of life—success, which has become a somewhat odious onion nowadays, chiefly because we so often give the name to the wrong thing. When you reach the evening of your days you will, I think, see—with, I hope, becoming cheerfulness—that we are all failures, at least all the best of us. The greatest Scotsman that ever lived wrote himself down a failure:

> The poor inhabitant below
> Was quick to learn and wise to know,
> And keenly felt the friendly glow
> And softer flame.
> But thoughtless follies laid him low,
> And stained his name.

75

Perhaps the saddest lines in poetry, written by a man who could make things new for the gods themselves.

If you want to avoid being like Burns there are several possible ways. Thus you might copy us, as we shine forth in our published memoirs, practically without a flaw. No one so obscure nowadays but that he can have a book about him. Happy the land that can produce such subjects for the pen.

But do not put your photograph at all ages into your autobiography. That may bring you to the ground. "My Life; and what I have done with it"; that is the sort of title, but it is the photographs that give what you have done with it. Grim things, those portraits; if you could read the language of them you would often find it unnecessary to read the book. The face itself, of course, is still more tell-tale, for it is the record of all one's past life. There the man stands in the dock, page by page; we ought to be able to see each chapter of him melting into the next like the figures in the cinematograph. Even the youngest of you has got through some chapters already. When you go home for the next vacation some one is sure to say "John has changed a little; I don't quite see in what way, but he has changed." You remember they said that last vacation. Perhaps it means that you look less like your father. Think that out. I could say some nice things of your betters if I chose.

In youth you tend to look rather frequently into a mirror, not at all necessarily from vanity. You say to yourself, "What an interesting face; I wonder what he is to be up to?" Your elders do not look into the mirror so often. We know what he has been up to. As yet there is unfortunately no science of reading other people's faces; I think a chair for this should be founded in St. Andrews.

The new professor will need to be a sublime philosopher, and for obvious reasons he ought to wear spectacles before his senior class. It will be a gloriously optimistic chair, for he can tell his students the glowing truth, that what their faces are to be like presently depends mainly on themselves. Mainly, not altogether—

I am the master of my fate,
I am the captain of my soul.

I found the other day an old letter from Henley that told me of the circumstances in which he wrote that poem. "I was a patient," he writes, "in the old infirmary of Edinburgh. I had heard vaguely of Lister, and went there as a sort of forlorn hope on the chance of saving my foot. The great surgeon received me, as he did and does everybody, with the greatest kindness, and for twenty months I lay in one or other ward of the old place under his care. It was a desperate business, but he saved my foot, and here I am." There he was, ladies and gentlemen, and what he was doing during that "desperate business" was singing that he was master of his fate.

If you want an example of courage try Henley. Or Stevenson. I could tell you some stories about these two, but they would not be dull enough for a rectorial address. For courage, again, take Meredith, whose laugh was "as broad as a thousand beeves at pasture." Take, as I think, the greatest figure literature has still left to us, to be added to-day to the roll of St. Andrews' alumni, though it must be in absence. The pomp and circumstance of war will pass, and all others now alive may fade from the scene, but I think the quiet figure of Hardy will live on.

I seem to be taking all my examples from the calling I was lately pretending to despise. I should like to read you some passages of a letter from a man of another calling, which I think will hearten you. I have the little filmy sheets here. I thought you might like to see the actual letter; it has been a long journey; it has been to the South Pole. It is a letter to me from Captain Scott of the Antarctic, and was written in the tent you know of, where it was found long afterwards with his body and those of some other very gallant gentlemen, his comrades. The writing is in pencil, still quite clear, though toward the end some of the words trail away as into the great silence that was waiting for them. It begins:

We are pegging out in a very comfortless spot. Hoping this letter may be found and sent to you, I write you a word of farewell. I want you to think well of me and my end." (After some private instructions too intimate to read, he goes on): "Goodbye—I am not at all afraid of the end, but sad to miss many a simple pleasure which I had planned for the future in our long marches . . . We are in a desperate state—feet frozen, etc., no fuel, and a long way from food, but it would do your heart good to be in our tent, to hear our songs and our cheery conversation . . ." (Later it is here that the words become difficult)—"We are very near the end . . . We did intend to finish ourselves when things proved like this, but we have decided to die naturally without."

I think it may uplift you all to stand for a moment by that tent and listen, as he says, to their songs and cheery conversation. When I think of Scott I remember the strange Alpine story of the youth who fell down a glacier and was lost, and of how a scientific companion, one of several who accompanied him, all young, computed that the body would again appear at a certain date and place many years afterwards. When that time came round some of the survivors returned to the glacier to see if the prediction would be fulfilled; all old men now; and the body reappeared as young as on the day he left them. So Scott and his comrades emerge out of the white immensities always young.

How comely a thing is affliction borne cheerfully, which is not beyond the reach of the humblest of us. What is beauty? It is these hardbitten men singing courage to you from their tent; it is the waves of their island home crooning of their deeds to you who are to follow them. Sometimes beauty boils over and then spirits are abroad. Ages may pass as we look or listen, for time is annihilated. There is a very old legend told to me by Nansen the explorer—I like well to be in the company of explorers—the legend of a monk who had wandered into the fields and a lark began to sing. He had never heard a lark before, and he stood there entranced until the bird and its song had become part of the heavens. Then he went back to the monastery and found there a doorkeeper whom he did not know and who did not know him. Other monks came, and they were all strangers to him. He told them he was Father Anselm, but that was no help. Finally they looked through the books of the monastery, and these revealed that there had been a Father Anselm there a hundred or more years before. Time had been blotted out while he listened to the lark.

That, I suppose, was a case of beauty boiling over, or a soul boiling over; perhaps the same thing. Then spirits walk.

They must sometimes walk St. Andrews. I do not mean the ghosts of queens or prelate; but one that keeps step, as soft as snow, with some poor student. He sometimes catches sight of it. That is why his fellows can never quite touch him, their best beloved; he half knows something of which they know nothing—the secret that is hidden in the face of the Mona Lisa. As I see him, life is so beautiful to him that its proportions are monstrous. Perhaps his childhood may have been overfull of gladness; they don't like that. If the seekers were kind he is the one for whom the flags of his college would fly one day. But the seeker I am thinking of is unfriendly, and so our student is "the lad that will never be old." He often gaily forgets, and thinks he has slain his foe by daring him, like him who, dreading water, was always the first to leap into it. One can see him serene, astride a Scotch cliff, singing to the sun the farewell thanks of a boy:

Throned on a cliff serene Man saw the sun
hold a red torch above the farthest seas,
and the fierce island pinnacles put on
in his defence their sombre panoplies;
Foremost the white mists eddied, trailed and
spun like seekers, emulous to clasp his knees,
till all the beauty of the scene seemed one,
led by the secret whispers of the breeze.
"The sun's torch suddenly flashed upon his face
and died; and he sat content in subject night
and dreamed of an old dead foe that had

sought and found him;
a beast stirred boldly in his resting-place;
And the cold came; Man rose to his masterheight,
shivered, and turned away; but the mists
were round him."

If there is any of you here so rare that the seekers have taken an ill-will to him, as to the boy who wrote those lines, I ask you to be careful. Henley says in that poem we were speaking of:

Under the bludgeonings of chance
My head is bloody but unbowed.

A fine mouthful, but perhaps "My head is bloody and bowed" is better. Let us get back to that tent with its songs and cheery conversations. Courage. I do not think it is to be got by your becoming solemn-sides before your time. You must have been warned against letting the golden hours slip by. Yes, but some of them are golden only because we let them slip. Diligence—ambition; noble words, but only if "touched to fine issues." Prizes may be dross, learning lumber, unless they bring you into the arena with increased understanding. Hanker not too much after worldly prosperity that corpulent cigar; if you became a millionaire you would probably go swimming around for more like a diseased goldfish. Look to it that what you are doing is not merely toddling to a competency. Perhaps that must be your fate, but fight it and then, though you fail, you may still be among the elect of whom we have spoken. Many a brave man has had to come to it at last. But there are the complacent toddlers from the start. Favour them not, ladies, especially now that every one of you carries a possible maréchal's baton under her gown. "Happy," it has been said by a distinguished man, "is he who can leave college with an unreproaching conscience and an unsullied heart." I don't know; he sounds to me like a sloppy, watery sort of fellow; happy, perhaps, but if there be red blood in him, impossible. Be not disheartened by ideals of perfection which can be achieved only by those who run away. Nature, that "thrifty goddess," never gave you "the smallest scruple of her excellence" for that. Whatever bludgeonings may be gathering for you, I think one feels more poignantly at your age than ever again in life. You have not our December roses to help you; but you have June coming, whose roses do not wonder, as do ours even while they give us their fragrance—wondering most when they give us most—that we should linger on an empty scene. It may indeed be monstrous but possibly courageous.

Courage is the thing. All goes if courage goes. What says our glorious Johnson of courage: "Unless a man has that virtue he has no security for preserving any other." We should thank our Creator three times daily for courage instead of for our bread, which, if we work, is surely the one thing we have a right to claim of Him. This courage is a proof of our immortality, greater even than gardens "when the eve is cool." Pray for it. "Who rises from prayer a better man, his prayer is answered." Be not merely courageous, but light-hearted and gay. There is an officer who was the first of our Army to land at Gallipoli. He was dropped overboard to light decoys on the shore, so as to deceive the Turks as to where the landing was to be. He pushed a raft containing these in front of him. It was a frosty night, and he was naked and painted black. Firing from the ships was going on all around. It was a two-hours' swim in pitch darkness. He did it, crawled through the scrub to listen to the talk of the enemy, who were so near that he could have shaken hands with them, lit his decoys and swam back. He seems to look on this as a gay affair. He is a V.C. now, and you would not think to look at him that he could ever have presented such a disreputable appearance. Would you? (indicating Colonel Freyberg).

Those men of whom I have been speaking as the kind to fill the fife could all be light-hearted on occasion. I remember Scott by Highland streams trying to rouse me by maintaining that haggis is boiled bagpipes; Henley in dispute as to whether, say, Turgenieff or Tolstoi could hang the other on his watch-chain; he sometimes clenched the argument by casting his crutch at you; Stevenson responded in the same gay spirit by giving that crutch to John Silver; you remember with what adequate results. You must cultivate this lightheartedness if you are to hang your betters on your watch-chains. Dr. Johnson—let us have him again—does not seem to have discovered in his travels that the Scotts are a light-hearted nation. Boswell took him to task for saying that the death of Garrick had eclipsed the gaiety of nations. "Well, sir," Johnson said, "there may be occasions when it is permissible to," etc. But Boswell would not let go. "I cannot see, sir, how it could in any case have eclipsed the gaiety of nations, as England was the only nation before whom he had ever played." Johnson was really stymied, but you would never have known it. "Well, sir," he said, holding out, "I understand that Garrick once played in Scotland, and if Scotland has any gaiety to eclipse, which, sir, I deny——."

Prove Johnson wrong for once at the Students' Union and in your other societies. I much regret that there was no Students' Union at Edinburgh in my time. I hope you are fairly noisy and that members are sometimes led out. Do you keep to the old topics? King Charles's head; and Bacon wrote Shakespeare, or if he did not he missed the opportunity of his life. Don't forget to speak scornfully of the Victorian age; there will be time for meekness when you try to better it. Very soon you will be Victorian or that sort of thing yourselves; next session probably, when the freshmen come up. Afterwards, if you go in for my sort of calling, don't begin by thinking you are the last word in art; quite possibly you are not; steady yourselves by remembering that there were great men before William K. Smith. Make merry while you may. Yet lightheartedness is not for ever and a day. At its best it is the gay companion of innocence; and when innocence goes as go it must—they soon trip off together, looking for something younger. But courage comes all the way:

> Fight on, my men, says Sir Andrew Barton,
> I am hurt, but I am not slaine;
> I'll lie me down and bleed a-while,
> And then I'll rise and fight againe.

Another piece of advice; almost my last. For reasons you may guess I must give this in a low voice. Beware of M'Connachie. When I look in a mirror now it is his face I see. I speak with his voice. I once had a voice of my own, but nowadays I hear it from far away only, a melancholy, lonely, lost little pipe. I wanted to be an explorer, but he willed otherwise. You will all have your M'Connachies luring you off the high road. Unless you are constantly on the watch, you will find that he has slowly pushed you out of yourself and taken your place. He has rather done for me. I think in his youth he must somehow have guessed the future and been fleggit by it, flichtered from the nest like a bird, and so our eggs were left, cold. He has clung to me, less from mischief than for companionship; I half like him and his penny whistle; with all his faults he is as Scotch as peat; he whispered to me just now that you elected him, not me, as your Rector.

A final passing thought. Were an old student given an hour in which to revisit the St. Andrews of his day, would he spend more than half of it at lectures? He is more likely to be heard clattering up bare stairs in search of old companions. But if you could choose your hour from all the five hundred years of this seat of learning, wandering at your will from one age to another, how would you spend it? A fascinating theme; so many notable shades at once astir that St. Leonard's and St. Mary's grow murky with them. Hamilton, Melville, Sharpe, Chalmers, down to Herkless, that distinguished Principal, ripe scholar and warm friend, the loss of whom I deeply deplore with you. I think if that hour were mine, and though at St. Andrews he was but a passerby, I would give a handsome part of it to a walk with Dr. Johnson. I should like to have the time of day passed to me in twelve languages by the Admirable Crichton. A wave of the hand to Andrew Lang; and then for the archery butts with the gay Montrose, all a-ruffled and ringed, and in the gallant St. Andrews studentmanner, continued as I understand to this present day, scattering largess as he rides along,

> But where is now the courtly troupe
> That once went riding by?
> I miss the curls of Canteloupe,
> The laugh of Lady Di.

We have still left time for a visit to a house in South Street, hard by St. Leonard's. I do not mean the house you mean. I am a Knox man. But little will that avail, for M'Connachie is a Queen Mary man. So, after all, it is at her door we chap, a last futile effort to bring that woman to heel. One more house of call, a student's room, also in South Street. I have chosen my student, you see, and I have chosen well; him that sang—

> Life has not since been wholly vain,
> And now I bear
> Of wisdom plucked from joy and pain
> Some slender share.
>
> But howsoever rich the store,
> I'd lay it down
> To feel upon my back once more
> The old red gown.

Well, we have at last come to an end. Some of you may remember when I began this address; we are all older now. I thank you for your patience. This is my first and last public appearance, and I never could or would have made it except to a gathering of Scottish students. If I have concealed my emotions in addressing you it is only the thrawn national way that deceives everybody except Scotsmen. I have not been as dull as I could have wished to be; but looking at your glowing faces cheerfulness and hope would keep breaking through. Despite the imperfections of your betters we leave you a great inheritance, for which others will one day call you to account. You come of a race of men the very wind of whose name has swept to the ultimate seas. Remember—

> Heaven doth with us as we with torches do,
> Not light them for themselves. . . .

Mighty are the Universities of Scotland, and they will prevail. But even in your highest exultations never forget that they are not four, but five. The greatest of them is the poor, proud homes you come out of, which said so long ago: "There shall be education in this land." She, not St. Andrews, is the oldest University in Scotland, and all the others are her whelps.

In bidding you good-bye, my last words must be of the lovely virtue. Courage, my children, and "greet the unseen with a cheer." "Fight on, my men," said Sir Andrew Barton. Fight on—you—for the old red gown till the whistle blows.

❧

Invictus
William Ernest Henley
(1849–1903)

OUT OF the night that covers me,
  Black as the pit from pole to pole,
I thank whatever gods may be,
  For my unconquerable soul.

In the fell clutch of circumstance
  I have not winced nor cried aloud.
Under the bludgeonings of chance
  My head is bloody but unbowed.

Beyond this place of wrath and tears
  Looms but the horror of the shade,
And yet the menace of the years
  Finds and shall find me unafraid.

It matters not how strait the gate
  How charged with punishments the scroll,
I am the master of my fate,
  I am the captain of my soul.

If

Rudyard Kipling
(1865–1936)

IF YOU can keep your head when all about you
    Are losing theirs and blaming it on you,
If you can trust yourself when all men doubt you,
    But make allowances for their doubting too;
If you can wait and not be tired by waiting,
    Or being lied about, don't deal in lies,
Or being hated, don't give way to hating,
    And yet don't look too good, nor talk too wise:

If you can dream and not make dreams your master;
    If you can think—and not make thoughts your aim;
If you can meet with Triumph and Disaster
    And treat those two imposters just the same;
If you can bear to hear the truth you've spoken
    Twisted by knaves to make a trap for fools,
Or watch the things you gave your life to, broken,
    And stoop and build 'em up with worn-out tools:

If you can make one heap of all your winnings
    And risk it on one turn of pitch-and-toss,
And lose, and start again at your beginnings
    And never breathe a word about your loss;

If you can force your heart and nerve and sinew
    To serve your turn long after they are gone,
And so hold on when there is nothing in you
    Except the Will which says to them: "Hold on!"

If you can talk with crowds and keep your virtue,
    Or walk with Kings—nor lose the common touch,
If neither foes nor loving friends can hurt you;
    If all men count with you, but none too much;
If you can fill the unforgiving minute
    With sixty seconds' worth of distance run,
Yours is the Earth and everything that's in it,
    And—which is more—you'll be a Man, my son!

The Bridge Builder

Will Allen Dromgoole (d. 1934)

AN OLD MAN going a lone highway
Came at the evening, cold and gray,
To a chasm vast and wide and steep,
With waters rolling cold and deep.

The old man crossed in the twilight dim,
The sullen stream had no fears for him;
But he turned when safe on the other side,
And built a bridge to span the tide.

"Old man," said a fellow pilgrim near,
"You are wasting your strength with building here.
Your journey will end with the ending day,
You never again will pass this way.
You've crossed the chasm, deep and wide,
Why build you this bridge at eventide?"

The builder lifted his old gray head.
"Good friend, in the path I have come," he said,
"There followeth after me today
A youth whose feet must pass this way.
The chasm that was as nought to me
To that fair-haired youth may a pitfall be;
He, too, must cross in the twilight dim—
Good friend, I am building this bridge for him."

"ACRES OF DIAMONDS" is the title of a speech given by Russell H. Conwell in the latter half of the nineteenth century. Records show that it was delivered over six thousand times in all parts of the country.

Full of Yankee sagacity and values, the speech proclaims that opportunity is waiting everywhere and all the time.

Some authorities have suggested that this speech helped create the American free enterprise system. It could very well have had that impact; Dr. Conwell was immensely popular and attracted large crowds.

Following service in the Civil War, Dr. Conwell had a distinguished career as a down-to-earth speaker and preacher in Philadelphia, Pennsylvania. He was the founder and first president of Temple University.

Acres of Diamonds

Russell H. Conwell (1843–1925)

WHEN GOING DOWN the Tigris and Euphrates rivers many years ago with a party of English travelers I found myself under the direction of an Arab guide whom we hired at Baghdad. He thought that it was not only his duty to guide us down those rivers, and do what he was paid for doing, but also to entertain us with stories curious and weird, ancient and modern, strange and familiar. Many of them I have forgotten, but there is one I shall never forget.

"I will tell you a story now which I reserve for my particular friends." When he emphasized the words "particular friends," I listened and I have ever been glad I did. There once lived not far from the River Indus an ancient Persian by the name of Ali Hafed. He said that Ali Hafed owned a very large farm, that he had orchards, grain fields, and gardens; that he had money at interest, and was a wealthy and contented man. He was contented because he was wealthy, and wealthy because he was contented.

One day there visited that old Persian farmer one of those ancient Buddhist priests, one of the wise men of the East. He sat down by the fire and told the old farmer how this world of ours was made. He said that this world was once a mere bank of fog, and that the Almighty thrust His finger into this bank of fog, and began slowly to move His finger around, increasing the speed until at last He whirled this bank of fog into a solid ball of fire. Then it went rolling through the universe, burning its way through other banks of fog, and condensed the moisture without, until it fell in floods of rain upon its hot surface, and cooled the outward crust. Then the internal fires bursting outward through the crust threw up the mountains and hills, the valleys, the plains and prairies of this wonderful world of ours. If this internal molten mass came bursting out and cooled very quickly it became granite; less quickly copper, less quickly silver, less quickly gold, and, after gold, diamonds were made.

Said the old priest, "A diamond is a congealed drop of sunlight." Now that is literally scientifically true, that a diamond is an actual deposit of carbon from the sun. The old priest told Ali Hafed that if he had one diamond the size of his thumb he could purchase the country, and if he had a mine of diamonds he could place his children upon thrones through the influence of their great wealth.

Ali Hafed heard all about diamonds, how much they were worth, and went to his bed that night a poor man. He had not lost anything, but he was poor because he was discontented, and discontented because he feared he was poor. He said, "I want a mine of diamonds," and he lay awake all night.

Early in the morning he sought out the priest. Ali Hafed said to him: "Will you tell me where I can find diamonds?"

"Diamonds! What do you want with diamonds?" "Why, I wish to be immensely rich." "Well, then, go along and find them. That is all you have to do; go and find them, and then you have them." "But I don't know where to go." "Well, if you will find a river that runs through white sands, between high mountains, in those white sands you will always find diamonds." "I don't believe there is any such river." "Oh yes, there are plenty of them. All you have to do is to go and find them, and then you have them." Said Ali Hafed, "I will go."

So he sold his farm, collected his money, left his family in charge of a neighbor, and away he went in search of diamonds. He began his search at the Mountains of the Moon. Afterward he came around into Palestine, then wandered on into Europe, and at last when his money was well spent and he was in rags, wretchedness, and poverty, he stood on the shore of that bay at Barcelona, in Spain, when a great tidal wave came rolling in between the pillars of Hercules, and the poor, afflicted, suffering, dying man could not resist the awful temptation to cast himself into that incoming tide, and he sank beneath its foaming crest, never to rise in this life again.

When that old guide had told me that awfully sad story he stopped the camel I was riding on and went back to fix the baggage that was coming off another camel, and I had an opportunity to muse over his story while he was gone. I remember saying to myself, "Why did he reserve that story for his 'particular friends'?" There seemed to be no beginning, no middle, no end, nothing to it. That was the first story I had ever heard told in my life, and would be the first one I ever read, in which the hero was killed in the first chapter. I had but one chapter of that story, and the hero was dead.

When the guide came back and took up the halter of my camel, he went right ahead with the story, into the second chapter, just as though there had been no break. The man who purchased Ali Hafed's farm one day led his camel into the garden to drink, and as that camel put its nose into the shallow water of that garden brook, Ali Hafed's successor noticed a curious flash of light from the white sands of the stream. He pulled out a black stone having an eye of light reflecting all the hues of the rainbow. He took the pebble into the house and put it on the mantel which covers the central fires, and forgot all about it.

A few days later this same old priest came in to visit Ali Hafed's successor, and the moment he opened that drawing room door he saw that flash of light on the mantel, and he rushed up to it, and shouted: "Here is a diamond! Has Ali Hafed returned?" "Oh no, Ali Hafed has not returned, and that is not a diamond. That is nothing but a stone we found right out here in our own garden." "But," said the priest, "I tell you I know a diamond when I see it. I know positively that is a diamond."

Then together they rushed out into that old garden and stirred up the white sands with their fingers, and lo! there came up other more beautiful and valuable gems than the first. "Thus," said the guide to me, and, friends, it is historically true, "was discovered the most magnificent diamond mine in all the history of mankind, excelling the Kimberly itself. The Kohinoor, and the Orloff of the crown jewels of England and Russia, the largest on earth, came from that mine."

When that old Arab guide told me the second chapter of his story, he then took off his Turkish cap and swung it around in the air again to get my attention to the moral. As he swung his hat, he said, "Had Ali Hafed remained at home and dug in his own cellar, or underneath his own wheat fields, or in his own garden, instead of wretchedness, starvation, and death by suicide in a strange land, he would have had 'acres of diamonds.' For every acre of that old farm, yes, every shovelful, afterward revealed gems which since have decorated the crowns of monarchs."

When he had added the moral to his story I saw why he reserved it for "his particular friends." But I did not tell him I could see it. It was that mean old Arab's way of going around a thing like a lawyer, to say indirectly what he did not dare say directly, that "in his private opinion there was a certain young man then traveling down the Tigris River that might better be at home in America." I did not tell him I could see that, but I told him his story reminded me of one, and I told it to him quick, and I think I will tell it to you.

I told him of a man out in California in 1847, who owned a ranch. He heard they had discovered gold in southern California, and so with a passion for gold he sold his ranch to Colonel Sutter, and away he went, never to come back. Colonel Sutter put a mill upon a stream that ran through that ranch, and one day his little girl brought some wet sand from the raceway into their home and sifted it through her fingers before the fire, and in that falling sand a visitor saw the first shining scales of real gold that were ever discovered in California. The man who had owned the ranch wanted gold, and he could have secured it for the mere taking. Indeed, thirty-eight millions of dollars has been taken out of a very few acres since then. About eight years ago I delivered this lecture in a city that stands on that farm, and they told me that a one-third owner for years and years had been getting one hundred and twenty dollars in gold every fifteen minutes, sleeping or waking.

But a better illustration really than that occurred here in our own Pennsylvania. If there is anything I enjoy above another on the platform, it is to get one of these German audiences in Pennsylvania before me, and fire that at them, and I enjoy it tonight. There was a man living in Pennsylvania, not unlike some Pennsylvanians you have seen who owned a farm, and he did with that farm just what I should do with a farm if I owned one in Pennsylvania—he sold it. But before he sold it he decided to secure employment collecting coal oil for his cousin, who was in the business in Canada, where they first discovered oil on this continent. They dipped it from the running streams at that early time. So this Pennsylvania farmer wrote to his cousin asking for employment. You see, friends, this farmer was not altogether a foolish man. No, he was not. He did not leave his farm until he had something else to do. *Of all the simpletons the stars shine on I don't know of a worse one than the man who leaves one job before he has gotten another*. When he wrote to his cousin for employment, his cousin replied, "I cannot engage you because you know nothing about the oil business."

Well, then the old farmer said, "I will know," and with most commendable zeal he set himself to the study of the whole subject. He began away back at the second day of God's creation when this world was covered thick and deep with that rich vegetation which since has turned to the primitive beds of coal. He studied the subject until he found that the drainings really of those rich beds of coal furnished the coal oil that was worth pumping, and then he found how it came up with the living springs. He studied until he knew what it looked like, smelled like, tasted like, and how to refine it. Now said he in his letter to his cousin, "I understand the oil business." His cousin answered, "All right, come on."

So he sold his farm, according to the county record, for $833 (even money, "no cents"). He had scarcely gone from that place before the man who purchased the spot went out to arrange for the watering of the cattle. He found the previous owner had gone out years before and put a plank across the brook back of the barn, edgewise into the surface of the water just a few inches. The purpose of that plank at that sharp angle across the brook was to throw over to the other bank a dreadful-looking scum through which the cattle would not put their noses. But with that plank there to throw it all over to one side, the cattle would drink below, and thus that man who had gone to Canada had been himself damming back for twenty-three years a flood of coal oil which the state geologists of Pennsylvania declared to us ten years later was even then worth a hundred millions of dollar to our state, and four years ago our geologists declared the discovery to be worth to our state a thousand millions of dollars. The man who owned that territory on which the city of Titusville now stands, and those Pleasantville valleys, had studied the subject from the second day of God's creation clear down to the present time. He studied it until he knew all about it, and yet he is said to have sold the whole of it for $833, and again I say, "no sense."

But I need another illustration. I found it in Massachusetts, and I am sorry I did because that is the state I came from. This young man in Massachusetts furnishes just another phase of my thought. He went to Yale College and studied mines and mining, and became such an adept as a mining engineer that he was employed by the authorities of the university to train students who were behind in their classes. During his senior year he earned $15 a week for doing that work. When he graduated they raised his pay from $15 to $45 a week, and offered him a professorship, and as soon as they did he went right home to his mother. *If they had raised that boy's pay from $15 to $15.60 he would have stayed and been proud of the place, but when they put it up to $45 at one leap, he said, "Mother, I won't work for $45 a week. The idea of man with a brain like mine working for $45 a week!* Let's go to California and stake out gold mines and silver mines, and be immensely rich."

Said his mother, "Now, Charlie, it is just as well to be happy as it is to be rich."

"Yes," said Charlie, "but it is just as well to be rich and happy, too." And they were both right about it. As he was an only son and she a widow, of course he had his way. They always do.

They sold out in Massachusetts, and instead of going to California, they went to Wisconsin, where he went into the employ of the Superior Copper Mining Company at $15 a week again, but with the proviso in his contract that he should have an interest in any mines he should discover for the company.

He had scarcely gotten out of the old homestead before the succeeding owner went out to dig potatoes. The potatoes were already growing in the ground when he bought the farm, and as the old farmer was bringing in a basket of potatoes it hugged very tight to the ends of the stone fence. When that basket hugged so tight he set it down on the ground, and then dragged on one side, and pulled on the other side, and this farmer noticed in the upper and outer corner of that stone wall, right next the gate, a block of native silver eight inches square. That professor of mines, mining, and mineralogy who knew so much about the subject that he would not work for $45 a week, when he sold that homestead in Massachusetts sat right on that silver.

My friends, that mistake is very universally made, and why should we even smile at him. I often wonder what has become of him.

As I come here tonight and look around this audience I am seeing again what through these fifty years I have continually seen—men that are making precisely that same mistake. I say to you that you have "acres of diamonds" in Philadelphia right where you now live. "Oh," but you will say, "you cannot know much about our city if you think there are any 'acres of diamonds' here." But if you do not have the actual diamond mines literally you have all that would be good for you to have.

Again I say that the opportunity to get rich, to attain unto great wealth, is here in Philadelphia now, within the reach of almost every man and woman who hears me speak tonight, and I mean just what I say. I have not come to this platform to recite something to you. I have come to tell you what is in God's sight I believe to be the truth, and if the years of life have been of any value to me in the attainment of common sense, I know I am right; that the men and women sitting here have within their reach "acres of diamonds." There never was a place on earth more adapted than the city of Philadelphia today, and never in the history of the world did a poor man without capital have such an opportunity to get rich quickly and honestly as he has now in our city. I say it is the truth, and I want you to accept it as such; for if you think I have come to simply recite something that happened elsewhere, then I would better not be here. I have no time to waste in any such talk, but to say the things I believe, and unless some of you get richer for what I am saying tonight my time is wasted.

I say that you ought to get rich, and it is your duty to get rich. How many of my pious brethren say to me, "Do you, a Christian minister, spend your time going up and down the country advising young people to get rich, to get money?" "Yes, of course I do." They say, "Isn't that awful! Why don't you preach the gospel instead of preaching about man's making money?" "Because to make money honestly is to preach the gospel." That is the reason. The men who get rich may be the most honest men you find in the community.

"Oh," but says some young man here tonight, "I have been told all my life that if a person has money he is very dishonest and dishonorable and mean and contemptible." My friend, that is the reason why you have none, because you have that idea of people. The foundation of your faith is altogether false. Let me say here clearly, and say it briefly, though subject to discussion which I have not time for here, ninety-eight out of one hundred of the rich men of America are honest. That is why they are rich. That is why they are trusted with money. That is why they carry on great enterprises and find plenty of people to work with them. It is because they are honest men.

My friend, you take and drive me out into the suburbs of Philadelphia, and introduce me to the people who own their homes around this great city, those beautiful homes with gardens and flowers, those magnificent homes so lovely in their art, and I will introduce you to the very best people in character as well as in enterprise in our city, and you know I will.

Money is power, and you ought to be reasonably ambitious to have it. You ought because you can do more good with it than you could without it. Money printed your Bible, money builds your churches, money sends your missionaries, and money pays for preachers, and you would not have many of them, either, if you did not pay them.

I say, then, you ought to have money. If you can honestly attain riches in Philadelphia, it is your Christian and godly duty to do so. It is an awful mistake of these pious people to think you must be awfully poor in order to be pious.

Some men say, "Don't you sympathize with the poor people?" Of course I do, or else I would not have been lecturing these years. I won't give in but what I sympathize with the poor, but the number of poor who are to be sympathized with is very small. To sympathize with a man whom God has punished for his sins, thus to help him when God would still continue to a just punishment, is to do wrong, no doubt about it, and we do that more than we help those who are deserving. While we should sympathize with God's poor—that is, those who cannot help themselves—let us remember there is not a poor person in the United States who was not made poor by his own shortcomings, or by the shortcomings of someone else. It is all wrong to be poor, anyhow. Let us give in to that argument and pass that to one side.

A gentleman gets up back there, and says, "Don't you think there are some things in world that are better than money?" Of course I do. Some things in this world that are higher and sweeter and purer than money. Love is the grandest thing on God's earth, but fortunate the lover who has plenty of money. Money is power, money is force, money will do good as well as harm. In the hands of good men and women it could accomplish, and it has accomplished, good.

I heard a man get up in a prayer meeting in our city and thank the Lord he was "one of God's poor." Well, I wonder what his wife thinks about that? She earns all the money that comes into that house, and he smokes a part of that on the veranda. I don't want to see any more of the Lord's poor of that kind, and I don't believe the Lord does. And yet there are some people who think in order to be pious you must be awfully poor. That does not follow at all. While we sympathize with the poor, let us not teach a doctrine like that.

Yet the age is prejudiced against advising a Christian man from attaining unto wealth. The prejudice is so universal and the years are far enough back, I think, for me to safely mention that years ago up at Temple

University there was a young man in our theological school who thought he was the only pious student in that department. He came into my office one evening and sat down by my desk, and said to me: "Mr. President, I think it is my duty sir, to come in and labor with you." "What has happened now?" Said he, "I heard you say at the Academy, at the Pierce School commencement, that you thought it was an honorable ambition for a young man to desire to have wealth, and that you thought it made him temperate, made him anxious to have a good name, and made him industrious. You spoke about man's ambition to have money helping to make him a good man. Sir, I have come to tell you the Holy Bible says that 'money is the root of all evil.'"

I told him I had never seen it in the Bible, and advised him to go out into the chapel and get the Bible, and show me the place. So out he went, and soon stalked into my office with Bible open, with all the bigoted pride of the narrow sectarian, or of one who founds his Christianity on some misinterpretation of Scripture. He flung the Bible down on my desk, and fairly squealed into my ear: "There it is, Mr. President; you can read it for yourself." I said to him: "Take that Bible and read it yourself, and give the proper emphasis to it."

He took the Bible, and proudly read, "'The love of money is the root of all evil.'"

When he quoted it right, of course he quoted the absolute truth. "The *love* of money is the root of all evil." He who tries to attain unto it too quickly, or dishonestly, will fall into many snares, no doubt about that. The love of money. What is that? It is making an idol of money, and idolatry pure and simple everywhere is condemned by the Holy Scriptures and by man's common sense. The man that worships the dollar instead of thinking of the purposes for which it ought to be used, the man who idolizes simply money, the miser that hoards his money in the cellar, or hides it in his stocking, or refuses to invest it where it will do the world good, that man who hugs the dollar until the eagle squeals has in him the root of all evil.

I think I will leave that behind me now and answer the question of nearly all of you who are asking, "Is there opportunity to get rich in Philadelphia?" Well, now, how simple a thing it is to see where it is, and the instant you see where it is it is yours. Some old gentleman gets up back there and says, "Mr. Conwell, have you lived in Philadelphia for thirty-one years and don't know that the time has gone by when you can make anything in this city?" "No, I don't think it is." "Yes, it is; I have tried it." "What business are you in?" "I kept a store here for twenty years, and never made over a thousand dollars in the whole twenty years."

"Well, then, you can measure the good you have been to this city by what this city has paid you, because a man can judge very well what he is worth by what he received. If you have not made over a thousand dollars in twenty years in Philadelphia, it would have been better for Philadelphia if they had kicked you out of the city nineteen years and nine months ago. A man has no right to keep a store in Philadelphia twenty years and not make at least five hundred thousand dollars, even though it be a corner grocery uptown." You say, "You cannot make five thousand dollars in a store now." Oh, my friends, if you will just take only four blocks around you, and find out what the people want and what you ought to supply and set them down with your pencil, and figure up the profits you would make if you did supply them, you would very soon see it. There is wealth right within the sound of your voice.

Someone says: "You don't know anything about business. A preacher never knows a thing about business." Well, then, I will have to prove that I am an expert. I don't like to do this, but I have to do it because my testimony will not be taken if I am not an expert. My father kept a country store, and if there is any place under the stars where a man gets all sorts of experience in every kind of mercantile transactions, it is in the country store. I am not proud of my experience, but sometimes when my father was away he would leave me in charge of the store, though fortunately for him that was not very often. But this did occur many times, friends: A man would come in the store, and say to me, "Do you keep jackknives?" "No, we don't keep jackknives," and I went off whistling a tune. Why did I care about the man anyhow? Then another farmer would come in and say, "Do you keep jackknives?" "No, we don't keep jackknives." Then I went away and whistled another tune. Then a third man came in the door and said, "Do you keep jackknives?" "No, Why is every one around here asking for jackknives? Do you suppose we are keeping this store to supply the whole neighborhood with jackknives?" Do you carry on your store like that in Philadelphia? The difficulty was I had not then learned that the foundation of godliness and the foundation principle of success in business are both the same precisely. The man who says, "I cannot carry my religion into business" advertises himself either as being an imbecile in business, or on the road to bankruptcy, or a thief, one of the three, sure. He will fail within a very few years. He certainly will if he doesn't carry his religion into business. If I had been carrying on my father's store on a Christian plan, godly plan, I would have had a jackknife for the third man when he called for it. Then I would have actually done him a kindness, and I would have received a reward myself, which it would have been my duty to take.

There are some over-pious people who think if you take a profit on anything you sell that you are an unrighteous man. On the contrary, you would be a criminal to sell goods for less than they cost. You have no right to do that. You cannot trust a man with your money who cannot take care of his own. You cannot trust a man in your family who is not true to his own wife. You cannot trust a man in the world who does not begin with his own heart, his own character, and his own life.

The man over there who said he could not make anything in a store in Philadelphia has been carrying on his store on the wrong principle. Suppose I go into your store tomorrow morning and ask, "Do you know neighbor A, who lives one square away, at house No. 1240?" "Oh yes, I have met him. He deals here at the corner store." "Where did he come from?" "I don't know." "How many does he have in his family?" "I don't know." "What church does he go to?" "I don't know, and don't care. What are you asking all these questions for?"

If you had a store in Philadelphia would you answer me like that? If so, then you are conducting your business just as I carried on my father's business in Worthington, Massachusetts. You don't know where your neighbor came from when he moved to Philadelphia, and you don't care. If you had cared you would be a rich man now. If you had cared enough about him to take an interest in his affairs, to find out what he needed, you would have been rich. But you go through the world saying, "No opportunity to get rich," and there is the fault right at your own door.

But another young man gets up over there and says, "I cannot take up the mercantile business." (While I am talking to trade it applies to every occupation.) "Why can't you go into the mercantile business?" "Because I haven't any capital." Oh, the weak and dudish creature that can't see over its collar! It makes a person weak to see these little dudes standing around the corners and saying, "Oh, if I had plenty of capital, how rich I would get." "Young man, do you think you are going to get rich on capital?" "Certainly." Well, I say, "Certainly not." If your mother has plenty of money, and she will set you up in business, you will "set her up in business," supplying you with capital.

The moment a young man or woman gets more money than he or she has grown to by practical experience, that moment he has gotten a curse. It is no help to a young man or woman to inherit money. It is no help to your children to leave them money, but if you leave them education, if you leave them Christian and noble character, if you leave them a wide circle of friends, if you leave them an honorable name, it is far better than that they should have money. There is no class of people to be pitied so much as the inexperienced sons and daughters of the rich of our generation.

One of the best things in our life is when a young man has earned his own living, and when he becomes engaged to some lovely young woman, and makes up his mind to have a home of his own. Then with that same love comes also that divine inspiration toward better things, and he begins to save his money. He begins to leave off his bad habits and put money in the bank. When he has a few hundred dollars he goes out in the suburbs to look for a home. He goes to the savings bank, perhaps, for half of the value, and then goes for his wife, and when he takes his bride over the threshold of that door for the first time he says in words of eloquence my voice can never touch: "I have earned this home myself. It is all mine, and I divide with thee." That is the grandest moment a human heart may ever know.

But a rich man's son can never know that. He takes his bride into a finer mansion, it may be, but he is obliged to go all the way through it and say to his wife, "My mother gave me that, my mother gave me that, and my mother gave me this," until his wife wishes she had married his mother. I pity the rich man's son.

The statistics of Massachusetts showed that not one rich man's son out of seventeen ever dies rich. I pity the rich man's sons unless they have the good sense of the elder Vanderbilt, which sometimes happens. He went to his father and said, "Did you earn all your money?" "I did, my son. I began to work on a ferry boat for twenty-five cents a day." "Then," said the son, "I will have none of your money," and he, too, tried to get employment on a ferry boat that Saturday night. He could not get one there, but he did get a place for three dollars a week.

Of course, if a rich man's son will do that, he will get the discipline of a poor boy that is worth more than a university education to any man. He would then be able to take care of the millions of his father. But as a rule the rich men will not let their sons do the very thing that made them great. As a rule, the rich man will not allow his son to work—and his mother!

Why, she would think it was a social disgrace if her poor, weak, little lily-fingered, sissy sort of a boy had to earn his living with honest toil. I have no pity for such rich men's sons.

At a banquet here in Philadelphia there sat beside me a kindhearted young man, and he said, "Mr. Conwell, you have been sick for two or three years. When you go out, take my limousine, and it will take you up to your house on Broad Street." I thanked him very much, and perhaps I ought not to mention the incident in this way, but I follow the facts. I got on to the seat with the driver of that limousine, outside, and when we were going up I asked the driver, "How much did this limousine cost?" "Six thousand eight hundred, and he had to pay the duty on it." "Well," I said, "does the owner of this machine ever drive it himself?" At that the chauffeur laughed so heartily that he lost control of his machine. He was so surprised at the question that he ran up on the sidewalk, and around a corner lamppost out into the street again. And when he got out into the street he laughed till the whole machine trembled. He said: "He drive this machine! Oh, he would be lucky if he knew enough to get out when we get there."

I must tell you about a rich man's son at Niagara Falls. I came in from the lecture to the hotel, and as I approached the desk of the clerk there stood a millionaire's son from New York. He was an indescribable specimen of anthropologic potency. He had a skullcap on one side of his head, with a gold tassel in the top of it, and a gold-headed cane under his arm with more in it than in his head. It is a very difficult thing to describe that young man. He wore an eyeglass that he could not see through, patent-leather boots that he could not walk in, and pants that he could not sit down in—dressed like a grasshopper.

This human cricket came up to the clerk's desk just as I entered, adjusted his unseeing eyeglass, and spake in this wise to the clerk. You see, he thought it was "Hinglist, you know," to lisp. "Thir, will you have the kindness to supply me with thome papah and enwelops!" The hotel clerk measured that man quick, and he pulled the envelopes and paper out of a drawer, threw them across the counter toward the young man, and then turned away to his books.

You should have seen that young man when those envelopes came across that counter. He swelled up like a gobbler turkey, adjusted his unseeing eyeglass and yelled: "Come right back here. Now thir, will you order a thervant to take that papah and enwelophs to yondah dethk." Oh, the poor, miserable, contemptible American monkey! He could not carry paper and envelopes twenty feet. I suppose he could not get his arms down to do it. I have no pity for such travesties upon human nature. If you have not capital, young man, I am glad of it. What you need is common sense, not copper cents.

The best thing I can do is to illustrate by actual facts well known to you all. A. T. Stewart, a poor boy in New York, had $1.50 to begin life on. He lost $87\frac{1}{2}$ cents of that on the very first venture. How fortunate that young man who loses the first time he gambles. That boy said, "I will never gamble again in business," and he never did. How came he to lose $87\frac{1}{2}$ cents? You probably all know the story how he lost it—because he bought some needles, threads, and buttons to sell which people did not want, and had them left on his hands, a dead loss. Said the boy, "I will not lose any more money in that way." Then he went around first to the doors and asked the people what they did want. Then when he had found out what they wanted he invested his $62^1/2$ cents to supply a known demand.

Study it wherever you choose—in business, in your profession, in your housekeeping, whatever your life, that one thing is the secret of success. You must first know the demand. You must first know what people need, and then invest yourself where you are most needed. A. T. Stewary went on that principle until he was worth what amounted afterward to forty millions of dollars, owning the very store in which Mr. Wanamaker carries on his great work in New York. His fortune was made by his losing something, which taught him the greatest lesson that he must only invest himself or his money in something that people need. When will you salesmen learn it? When will you manufacturers learn that you must know the changing needs of humanity if you would succeed in life? Apply yourselves, all you Christian people, as manufacturers or merchants or workmen to supply that human need. It is a great principle as broad as humanity and as deep as the Scripture itself.

The best illustration I ever heard was of John Jacob Astor. You know that he made the money of the Astor family when he lived in New York. He came across the sea in debt for his fare. But that poor boy with nothing in his pocket made a fortune of the Astor family on one principle. Some young man here tonight will say, "Well, they could make those fortunes over in New York, but they could not do it in Philadelphia!" My friends, did you ever read that wonderful book of Riis (his memory is sweet to us because of his recent death), wherein is given his statistical account of the records taken in 1889 of 107 millionaires of New York? If you read the account you will see that out of the 107 millionaires only seven made their money in New York. Out of the 107 millionaires worth ten million dollars in real estate then, 67 of them made their money in towns of less than 3,500 inhabitants. It makes not so much difference where you are as who you are. But if you cannot get rich in Philadelphia you certainly cannot do it in New York.

Now John Jacob Astor illustrated what can be done anywhere. He had a mortgage once on a millinery store, and they could not sell bonnets enough to pay the interest on his money. So he foreclosed that mortgage, took possession of the store, and went into partnership with the very same people, in the same store, with the same capital. He did not give them a dollar of capital. They had to sell goods to get any money.

Then he left them alone in the store just as they had been before, and he went out and sat down on a bench in the park in the shade. What was John Jacob Astor doing out there, and in partnership with people who had failed on his own hands? He had the most important and, to my mind, the most pleasant part of that partnership on his hands. For as John Jacob Astor sat on that bench he was watching the ladies as they went by; and where is the man who would not get rich at that business? As he sat on the bench if a lady passed him with her shoulders back and head up, and looked straight to the front, as if she did not care if all the world did gaze on her, then he studied her bonnet, and by the time it was out of sight he knew the shape of the frame, the color of the trimmings, and the crinklings in the feather. But in John Jacob Astor's day there was some art about the millinery business, and he went to the millinery store and said to them: "Now put into the show window just such a bonnet as I describe to you, because I have already seen a lady who likes such a bonnet. Don't make up any more until I come back." Then he went out and sat down again, and another lady passed him of a different form, of different complexion, with a different shape and color of bonnet. "Now," said he, "put such a bonnet as that in the show window." He did not fill his show window with a lot of hats and bonnets to drive people away, and then sit on the backstairs and bawl because people went to Wanamaker's to trade. He did not have a hat or a bonnet in that show window but what some lady liked before it was made up.

The tide of custom began immediately to turn in, and that has been the foundation of the greatest store in New York in that line, and still exists as one of three stores. Its fortune was made by John Jacob Astor after they had failed in business, not by giving them any more money, but by finding out what the ladies liked for bonnets before they wasted any material in making them up. I tell you if a man could foresee the millinery business he could foresee anything under heaven!

Suppose I were to go through this audience tonight and ask you in this great manufacturing city if there are not opportunities to get rich in manufacturing. "Oh yes," some young man says, "there are opportunities here still if you build with some trust and if you have two or three millions of dollars to begin with as capital." Young man, the history of the breaking up of the trusts that attach upon "big business" is only illustrating what is now the opportunity of the smaller man. The time never came in the history of the world when you get rich so quickly manufacturing without capital as you can now.

But you will say, "You cannot do anything of the kind. You cannot start without capital." Young man, let me illustrate for a moment. I must do it. It is my duty to every young man and woman, because we are all going into business very soon on the same plan. Young man, remember, if you know what people need you have gotten more knowledge of a fortune than any amount of capital can give you.

There was a poor man out of work living in Hingham, Massachusetts. He lounged around the house until one day his wife told him to get out and work, and, as he lived in Massachusetts, he obeyed his wife. He went out and sat down on the shore of the bay, and whittled a soaked shingle into a wooden chain. His children that evening quarreled over it, and he whittled a second one to keep peace.

While he was whittling the second one a neighbor came in and said: "Why don't you whittle toys and sell them? You could make money at that." "Oh," he said, "I would not know what to make." "Why don't you ask your own children right here in your own house what to make?" "What is the use of trying that?" said the man. "My children are different from other people's children." (I used to see people like that when I taught school.) But he acted upon the hint, and the next morning when Mary came down the stairway, he asked, "What do you want for a toy?" She began to tell him she would like a doll's bed, a doll's washstand, a doll's carriage, a little doll's umbrella, and went on with a list of things that would take him a lifetime to supply. So, consulting his own children, in his own house, he took the firewood, for he had no money to buy lumber, and whittled those strong, unpainted Hingham toys that were for so many years known all over the world.

That man began to make those toys for his own children, and then made copies and sold them through the boot-and-shoe store next door. He began to make a little money, and then a little more, and Mr. Lawson, in his *Frenzied Finance* says that man is the richest man in Massachusetts, and I think it is the truth. And that man is worth a hundred millions of dollars today, and has been only thirty-four years making it on that one principle—that one must judge that what his own children like at home other people's children would like in their homes, too; to judge the human heart by oneself, by one's wife or by one's children. It is the royal road to success in manufacturing. "Oh," but you say, "didn't he have any capital?" Yes, a penknife, but I don't know that he had paid for that.

I spoke thus to an audience in New Britain, Connecticut, and a lady four seats back went home and tried to take off her collar, and the collar button stuck in the buttonhole. She threw it out and said, "I am going to get something better than that to put on collars." Her husband said: "After what Conwell said tonight, you see there is a need of an improved collar fastener that is easier to handle. There is a human need; there is a great fortune. Now, then, get up a collar button and get rich." He made fun of her, and consequently made fun of me.

When her husband ridiculed her, she made up her mind she would make a better collar button, and when a woman makes up her mind "she will," and does not say anything about it, she does it. It was that New England woman who invented the snap button which you find anywhere now. It was first a collar button with a spring cap attached to the outer side. Any of you who wear modern waterproofs know the button that simply pushes together, and when you unbutton it you simply pull it apart. That is the button to which I refer, and which she invented. She afterward invented several other buttons, and then invested in more, and then was taken into partnership with great factories. Now that woman goes over the sea every summer in her private steamship—yes, and takes her husband with her! If her husband were to die, she would have money enough left now to buy a foreign duke or count for some such title as that at the latest quotations.

Now what is my lesson in that incident? It is this: I told her then, though I did not know her, what I now say to you. "Your wealth is too near to you. You are looking right over it"; and she had to look over it because it was right under her chin.

I have read in the newspaper that a woman never invented anything. Well, that newspaper ought to begin again. Of course, I do not refer to gossip—I refer to machines—and if I did I might better include the men. That newspaper could never appear if women had not invented something. Friends, think. Ye women, think! You say you cannot make a fortune because you are in some laundry, or running a sewing machine, it may be, or walking before some loom, and yet you can be a millionaire if you will but follow this almost infallible direction.

When you say a woman doesn't invent anything, I ask, who invented the Jacquard. The printer's roller, the printing press, were invented by farmer's wives. Who invented the cotton gin of the South that enriched our country so amazingly? Mrs. General Greene invented the cotton gin and showed the idea to Mr. Whitney, and he, like a man, seized it. Who was it that invented the sewing machine? If I would go to school tomorrow and ask your children they would say, "Elias Howe."

He was in the Civil War with me, and often in my tent, and I often heard him say that he worked fourteen years to get up that sewing machine. But his wife made up her mind one day that they would starve to death if there wasn't something or other invented pretty soon, and so in two hours she invented the sewing machine. Of course he took out the patent in his name. Men always do that. Who was it that invented the mower and the reaper? According to Mr. McCormick's confidential communications, so recently published, it was a West Virginia woman, who, after his father and he had failed altogether in making a reaper and gave it up, took a lot of shears and nailed them together on the edge of a board, with one shaft of each pair loose, and then wired them so that when she pulled the wire the other way it opened them, and there she had the principle of the mowing machine.

If you look at a mowing machine, you will see it is nothing but a lot of shears. If a woman can invent a mowing machine, if a woman can invent a Jacquard loom, if a woman can invent a cotton gin, if a woman can invent a trolley switch—as she did and made the trolleys possible; if a woman can invent, as Mr. Carnegie said, the great iron squeezers that laid the foundation of all the steel millions of the United States, "we men" can invent anything under the stars! I say that for the encouragement of the men.

Who are the great inventors of the world? Again this lesson comes before us. The great inventor sits next to you, or you are the person yourself. "Oh," but you will say, "I have never invented anything in my life." Neither did the great inventors until they discovered one great secret. Do you think it is a man with a head like a bushel measure or a man like a stroke of lightning? It is neither. The really great man is a plain, straightforward, everyday, common-sense man. You would not dream that he was a great inventor if you did not see something he had actually done. His neighbors do not regard him so great. You never see anything great over your back fence. You say there is no greatness among your neighbors. It is all away off somewhere else. Their greatness is ever so simple, so plain, so earnest, so practical, that the neighbors and friends never recognize it.

True greatness is often unrecognized. That is sure. You do not know anything about the greatest men and women. I went out to write the life of General Garfield, and a neighbor, knowing I was in a hurry, and as there was a great crowd around the front door, took me around to General Garfield's back door and shouted, "Jim! Jim!" And very soon "Jim" came to the door and let me in, and I wrote the biography of one of the grandest men of the nation, and yet he was just some old "Jim" to his neighbor. If you know a great man in Philadelphia and you should meet him tomorrow, you would say, "How are you, Sam?" or "Good morning, Jim." Of course you would. That is just what you would do.

One of my soldiers in the Civil War had been sentenced to death, and I went up to the White House in Washington—went there for the first time in my life—to see the President Abraham Lincoln. I went into the waiting room and sat down with a lot of others on the benches, and the secretary asked one after another to tell him what they wanted. After the secretary had been through the line, he went in, and then came back to the door and motioned for me. I went up to the anteroom, and the secretary said: "That is the President's door right over there. Just rap on it and go right in." I never was so taken aback, friends, in all my life, never. The secretary himself made it worse for me, because he had told me how to go in and then went out another door to the left and shut that.

There I was, in the hallway by myself before the President of the United States of America's door. I had been on fields of battle, where the shells did sometimes shriek and the bullets did sometimes hit me, but I always wanted to run. I have no sympathy with the old man who says, "I would just as soon march up to the cannon's mouth as eat my dinner." I have no faith in a man who doesn't know enough to be afraid when he is being shot at. I never was so afraid when the shells came around us at Antietam as I was when I went into that room that day; but I finally mustered the courage—I don't know how I ever did—and at arm's length tapped on the door. The man inside did not help me at all, but yelled out, "Come in and sit down!"

Well, I went in and sat down on the edge of a chair, and wished I were in Europe, and the man at the table did not look up. He was one of the world's greatest men, and was made great by one single rule. Oh, that all the great inventor or genius—invented the pin that now is called the safety pin, and out of that safety pin made the fortune of one of the great aristocratic families of this nation.

A poor man in Massachusetts who had worked in the nailworks was injured at thirty-eight, and he could earn but little money. He was employed in the office to rub out the marks on the bills made by pencil memorandums, and he used a rubber until his hand grew tired. He then tied a piece of rubber on the end of a stick and worked it like a plane. His little girl came and said, "Why, you have a patent, haven't you?" The father said afterward, "My daughter told me when I took that stick and put the rubber on the end that there was a patent, and that was the first thought of that." He went to Boston and applied for his patent, and every one of you that has a rubber-tipped pencil in your pocket is now paying tribute to the millionaire. He was once a poor man who thought—just thought.

⚜

A LITTLE BOOK, *I Dare You*, by William H. Danforth, who was founder and chairman of the board of the Ralston-Purina Company, has done me personally no end of good. My own copy is the twenty-ninth edition, privately printed; the book has touched thousands of lives.

To cite one case, *I Dare You* inspired sales of over $5 million worth of insurance in a special day of the Life Underwriters Association. It presents a fourfold program: "Think tall, Stand tall, Smile tall, Live tall." I knew the author personally, and he was a most inspiring person. His book has had huge sales among successful people.

Regretfully I can print here only a few pages of *I Dare You*.

123

What I've dared I've willed;
And what I've willed, I'll do!
Herman Melville (1819–1891)

❧

You Can Be Bigger Than You Are

William H. Danforth (1870–1955)

As a small boy, before the time of drainage ditches, I lived in the country surrounded by swamp lands. Those were days of chills and fever and malaria. When I came to the city to school, I was sallow-cheeked and hollow-cheated. One of my teachers, George Warren Krall, was what we then called a health crank. We laughed at his ideas. They went in one ear and came out the other. But George Warren Krall never let up. One day he seemed to single me out personally. With flashing eye and in tones that I will never forget, he looked straight at me and said, "I dare you to be the healthiest boy in the class."

That brought me up with a jar. Around me were boys all stronger and more robust than I. To be the healthiest boy in the class when I was thin and sallow and imagined at least that I was full of swamp poisons!—the man was crazy. But I was brought up to take dares. His voice went on. He

124

pointed directly at me. "I dare you to chase those chills and fevers out of your system. I dare you to fill your body with fresh air, pure water, wholesome food, and daily exercise until your cheeks are rosy, your chest full, and your limbs sturdy."

As he talked something seemed to happen inside me. My blood was up. It answered the dare and surged all through my body into tingling finger tips as though itching for battle.

I chased the poisons out of my system. I built a body that has equalled the strongest boys in that class, and has outlived and outlasted most of them. Since that day I haven't lost any time on account of sickness. You can imagine how often I have blessed that teacher who dared a sallow-cheeked boy to be the healthiest in the class.

Several years later, Henry Woods, one of our promising boys, pushed through the door of my office early one morning and stood facing me defiantly.

"I'm quitting," he said.

"What's the trouble, Henry?"

"Just this, I'm no salesman. I haven't got the nerve. I haven't got the ability, and I'm not worth the money you are paying me."

There was something splendid about the courage of a man who would so frankly admit failure to his boss. He couldn't do that without nerve. Suddenly my mind recalled the boyhood scene when a teacher dared a hollow-cheated youngster to be strong. To Henry's surprise, instead of accepting his resignation, I looked him squarely in the eye and said:

"If I know how to pick men, you have sales stuff in you. *I dare you,*

Henry Woods, to get out of this office, right now, and come back tonight with more orders than you have ever sold in any one day in your whole life."

He looked at me dumbfounded. Then a flash came into his eyes. It must have been the light of battle—the same something that had surged through me years before in answer to the teacher's dare. He turned and walked out of my office.

That night he came back. The defiant look of the early morning was replaced by the glow of victory. He had made the best record of his life. He had beaten his best—and he has been beating his best ever since. Incidentally, I'll give you a secret of his life. In his quiet way he is one of the best helpers of young salesmen I ever knew. He thrives by giving his experience to others. The world is full of men like Henry Woods just waiting for a Dare.

In the American Youth Foundation Camps each summer I come into contact with hundreds of young people who possess qualities of leadership. A few years ago a young fellow, who was working as a mechanic in a large electrical firm, came to me much perplexed. He had been forced to go to work when he had finished high school. Later he saw boys with technical college training outstrip him. Sensing he had ability to be much more than a mechanic, I dared him to leave his job and go back to school. Again I saw that priceless light of battle leap into the eyes of a fighter. He had no money, but, somehow, he got to college, was graduated with honors, and today the might-have-been mechanic is a prominent electrical engineer. I can tell you one of the secrets of his life, too . . . he keeps on growing by sharing, because now he has a mania for helping others get an education.

These are brief pages taken from the book of my practical experiences. There are scores of other pages like them. Unfortunately, however, there are many pages that would tell that other story of those who have been dared to do the super thing, but in whose eyes the light of battle failed to gleam. But the "I Dare You" plan *has* worked with thousands. It will work with you.

ARE YOU ONE OF THE PRICELESS FEW?

I am going to unfold a secret power that but few know how to use—the secret power of daring and sharing which carries with it tremendous responsibilities. Once you have it, you can never be the same again. Once it is yours, you can never rest until you have given it to others. And the more you give away the greater becomes your capacity to give. Deep down in the very fire of your being you must light an urge that can never be put out. It will catch this side of your life, then that side. It will widen your horizon. It will light up unknown reserves and discover new capacities for living and growing. It will become, if you don't look out, a mighty conflagration that will consume your every waking hour. And to its blazing glory a thousand other lives will come for light and warmth and power.

It is going to take courage to let this urge possess you. My life in business and my contacts with young people have convinced me that the world is full of unused talents and latent ability. The reason these talents lie buried is that the individual hasn't the courage to dig them up and use them. Everybody should be doing better than he is, but only a few dare. Prospectors for gold tell us that gold is where they find it. It may be in the bed of a river or on the mountain top. And prospectors for courage tell us the same thing. The one who dares may be found in a cottage or in a castle. But wherever you live, whoever you are, whatever you have or have not— if you dare, you are challenged to enlist in a great cause.

H. G. Wells tells how every human being can determine whether he has really succeeded in life. He says: "Wealth, notoriety, place, and power are no measure of success whatever. The only true measure of success is the ratio between what we might have done and what we might have been on the one hand, and the thing we have made and the thing we have made of ourselves on the other."

I want you to start a crusade in your life—to dare to be your best. I maintain that you are a better, more capable person than you have demonstrated so far. The only reason you are not the person you should be is you don't dare to be. Once you dare, once you stop drifting with the crowd and face life courageously, life takes on a new significance. New forces take shape within you. New powers harness themselves for your service.

Who wants to do unimportant and uninteresting things? Who even wants to gratify an ambition that has grown into a passion for fame and fortune? To desire something permanent in life, to develop your gifts to the largest possible use that's your dare. You have a wealth of possibilities, but maybe up to this time you have lacked a definite aim. You have a gun and plenty of ammunition. Now I dare you to aim at something worthy of the best that is in you.

My practical experience has convinced me that inner growth and broadening personality come from daring and sharing. You dare to use the talents you have. You find yourself growing stronger—physically, mentally, socially and spiritually. You multiply your daring a hundred-fold by sharing its fruits. You give your life away and, behold! a richer life comes back to you. This principle works through all of life:

Our most valuable possessions are those which can be shared without lessening: those which, when shared, multiply. Our least valuable possessions are those which, when divided, are diminished.

But how dare, you ask? First, it is necessary to agree that living aggressively changes the whole complexion of life. So many are preys to fear. You fear losing your job. You fear sickness or hard times or failure. But remember, courage is not the absence of fear, it is the conquest of it. Not until you dare to attack will you master your fears.

❧

Thought Conditioners

Norman Vincent Peale (b. 1898)

THE PLANE FROM New York rolled up to the gate at Chicago's O'Hare Airport, and passengers surged into the aisle. A man in back of me exclaimed, "Hey you," slapping me on my back and saying, "You saved my life." He pulled my booklet called *Thought Conditioners* out of his pocket. "With this!" he added.

The booklet was beat-up and frayed, showing much use. Indeed, it was so tattered that I said, "Well, I'm glad it benefited you, but let me send you a fresh copy."

"Nothing doing. This copy saved my life and I'm hanging on to it." So saying, he shook me by the hand vigorously. "Be seeing you," he said, and was lost in the crowd.

The booklet, *Thought Conditioners*, contains my favorite verses from the Bible, verses that have guided me personally through life. I wrote this booklet to share these verses with all who asked for them, and we have distributed free of charge more than five million copies! It's called *Thought Conditioners* for a special reason. Because success and happiness depend on certain kinds of thoughts that habitually pass through our minds, it is vital that we condition the mind with the right kind of mental activity; in other words, the right kind of thinking. One of the wisest men of all time was Marcus Aurelius, who said, "Our life is what our thoughts make of it."

Just as air-conditioning can make the air in a room crisp and healthy, so thought conditioning can make the mind alert and powerful enough to change the thinking that comes up from the subconscious mind, a creative kind of thinking that leads to success and happiness.

The Bible states in the following verse what its thoughts will do: "If ye abide in me, and my words abide in you, ye shall ask what ye will, and it shall be done unto you" (John 15:7).

Thought conditioning is an action technique. You may read these verses and say to yourself, "Yes, I see what is suggested," and simply let it go at that. But then they will make very little difference in your life.

On the other hand, if you take forty days and memorize one statement each day, repeating it morning, noon, and night so it is lodged in your memory, a wonderful thing will happen. When stress or temptation or failure or success comes, your mind will automatically release to your consciousness the appropriate verse to steer your thoughts and action in the right direction. This is called guidance. The way it happens is almost miraculous. I know it works, and millions of others will agree. This is what is meant by an action technique.

I earnestly hope that you will try it. Your thought processes will become strong, healthy, and successful.

I have included here only the Bible verses. The entire booklet contains a paragraph with each verse suggesting how it may be applied in your everyday life with its problems and successes. If you are interested in having the *Thought Conditioners* booklet, you may write for a free copy to Peale Center for Christian Living, 66 East Main Street, Pawling, New York 12564. Ask for booklet no. 15002.

1. Peace I leave with you, my peace I give unto you: not as the world giveth, give I unto you. Let not your heart be troubled, neither let it be afraid. (John 14:27)
2. The things which are impossible with men are possible with God. (Luke 18:27)
3. Renew a right spirit within me. (Psalm 51:10)
4. Come unto Me, all ye that labor and are heavy laden, and I will give you rest. (Matthew 11:28)
5. What things soever ye desire, when ye pray, believe that ye receive them, and ye shall have them. (Mark 11:24)
6. Trust in the Lord with all thine heart; and lean not unto thine own understanding. (Proverbs 3:5)

7. I am come that they might have life, and that they might have it more abundantly. (John 10:10)

8. Confess your faults one to another, and pray one for another, that ye may be healed. The effectual fervent prayer of a righteous man availeth much. (James 5:16)

9. If God be for us, who can be against us? (Romans 8:31)

10. The kingdom of God is within you. (Luke 17:21)

11. For God hath not given us the spirit of fear; but of power, and of love, and of a sound mind. (II Timothy 1:7)

12. Thou shalt guide me with Thy counsel, and afterward receive me to glory. (Psalm 73:24)

13. Wherefore take unto you the whole armor of God, that ye may be able to withstand in the evil day, and having done all to stand. (Ephesians 6:13)

14. God is our refuge and strength, a very present help in trouble. (Psalm 46:1)

15. He that handleth a matter wisely shall find good: and whoso trusteth in the Lord, happy is he. (Proverbs 16:20)

16. Incline your ear, and come unto Me: hear, and your soul shall live. (Isaiah 55:3)

17. Now unto him that is able to do exceeding abundantly above all that we ask or think, according to the power that worketh in us. (Ephesians 3:20)

18. Ask, and it shall be given you; seek, and ye shall find; knock, and it shall be opened unto you. (Matthew 7:7)

19. I have learned, in whatsoever state I am, therewith to be content. (Philippians 4:11)
20. My soul, wait thou only upon God; for my expectation is from Him. (Psalm 62:5)
21. Be strong and of a good courage; be not afraid, neither be thou dismayed: for the Lord thy God is with thee withersoever thou goest. (Joshua 1:9)
22. Be ye transformed by the renewing of your mind. (Romans 12:2)
23. But as many as received Him, to them gave He power. (John 1:12)
24. The thing which I greatly feared is come upon me, and that which I was afraid of is come unto me. (Job 3:25)
25. This one thing I do, forgetting those things which are behind, and reaching forth unto those things where are before, I press toward the mark for the prize of the high calling of God in Christ Jesus. (Philippians 3:13, 14)
26. In all these things we are more than conquerors through Him that loved us. For I am persuaded, that neither death, nor life, nor angels, nor principalities, nor powers, nor things present, nor things to come, nor height, nor depth, nor any other creature, shall be able to separate us from the love of God, which is in Christ Jesus our Lord. (Romans 8:37–39)
27. If any man thirst, let him come unto Me, and drink. (John 7:37)
28. Love your enemies, bless them that curse you, do good to them that hate you, and pray for them which despitefully use you, and persecute you. (Matthew 5:44)

29. I can do all things through Christ which strengtheneth me. (Philippians 4:13)

30. In Him we live, and move, and have our being. (Acts 17:28)

31. If any man be in Christ, he is a new creature: old things are passed away; behold all things are become new. (II Corinthians 5:17)

32. Whosoever shall say unto this mountain, be thou removed, and be thou cast into the sea; and shall not doubt in his heart, but shall believe that those things which he saith shall come to pass; he shall have whatsoever he saith. (Mark 11:23)

33. They that wait upon the Lord shall renew their strength; they shall mount up with wings as eagles; they shall run and not be weary; and they shall walk and not faint. (Isaiah 40:31)

34. Eye hath not seen, nor ear heard, neither have entered into the heart of man, the things which God hath prepared for them that love Him. (I Corinthians 2:9)

35. Cast thy burden upon the Lord, and He shall sustain thee: He shall never suffer the righteous to be moved. (Psalm 55:22)

36. Thou wilt keep him in perfect peace, whose mind is stayed on Thee. (Isaiah 26:3)

37. This is the refreshing. (Isaiah 28:12)

38. I sought the Lord, and He heard me, and delivered me from all my fears. (Psalm 34:4)

39. When ye stand praying, forgive, if ye have ought against any. (Mark 11:25)

40. They shall hunger no more, neither thirst any more; neither shall the sun light on them, nor any heat. For the lamb which is in the midst of the throne shall feed them, and shall lead them unto living fountains of waters: and God shall wipe away all tears from their eyes. (Revelation 7:16–17)

I CLOSE THIS BOOK with an account of the end of the great war between brothers, called by the North the Civil War and by the South of our long-healed country the War Between the States.

It is from a wonderful book, A *Dual Biography, Lee and Grant,* by Gene Smith. The author wrote of the two opposing generals with utter fairness and admiration for both.

Because I grew up in southern Ohio and used to watch the final defeat by death of the old veterans of the northern army and cherished my many friends of the South, I naturally have a fondness for the classic and heroic story of the Blue and the Gray.

Lee and Grant at Appomattox

Gene Smith (b. 1929)

LEE AND GRANT met face to face only four times; once during the Mexican War, when one of them was an illustrious staff officer and the other a lowly lieutenant; twice at the end of the Civil War, when each stood at the head of a great army; once in the White House, when one of them was President of the United States and the other the president of an obscure college. Only four times. Yet their names are linked forever in history—Robert E. Lee and Ulysses S. Grant.

This is the dramatic story of those two towering figures. It is the story of who they were as boys; as ardent young soldiers; as tender suitors of their wives-to-be; as husbands, fathers, generals.

Two men from two very different worlds.

And when their armies clashed, the earth shook and America held its breath. . . .

Off to the west, Grant tracked Robert Lee. To avoid getting entangled in rearguard skirmishes, he pushed his men on a parallel course south of Lee's, artillery horses shouldering the infantry off the roads, wagon trains rocking in the rear, the whole a mass of rushing men and horses running a race in the Virginia springtime.

Lee sped on, heading for the town of Amelia Court House some forty miles away, where trainloads of supplies had been directed. He was arrow-straight in the saddle, his face as calm as though he were watching the dress parade of a victorious army instead of a fleeing horde of smashed formations and broken regiments. He came to Amelia Court House with thirty thousand hungry men and found boxes of ammunition—but nothing to eat. The trainloads of food, mistakenly sent on to Richmond, were now in Federal hands. He took the news with no show of emotion, but from then on there was a haggard look on his face.

Twenty-five miles to the south, Grant was handed a dispatch from Sheridan saying he had intercepted the route Lee would have to take west out of Amelia Court House. The news was read to the troops, who wildly cheered it.

In the morning Sheridan struck Confederate columns on the move at Sayler's Creek and captured three thousand Confederates, including Custis Lee. And aide rode up and told Robert Lee that the wagon train had also been captured. Lee turned to General William Mahone, who was riding with him. "General, I have no other troops. Will you take your division to Sayler's Creek?"

He rode ahead with Mahone, the shrunken division following, and came to a high ridge overlooking the creek. Running up the ridge toward him were teamsters who had lost their wagons, soldiers who had thrown away their rifles—a routed mob.

"My God!" he cried. "Has the army been dissolved?" He went forward, seized a battle flag and, alone, on Traveller, held it up. Some of the men kept running, but others halted and formed with Mahone's division. The bunting blew itself around Lee's motionless figure. "I wish to fight here," he said.

"General Lee! Uncle Robert! Where's the man who won't follow Uncle Robert?" his soldiers shouted back; and they fought.

Ulysses Grant walked up the steps of a hotel in Farmville and wrote a note to General Lee:

> General:
>
> The result of the last week must convince you of the hopelessness of further resistance. I feel it is so, and regard it as my duty to shift from myself the responsibility of any further effusion of blood, by asking of you the surrender of that portion of the C. S. Army known as the Army of Northern Virginia.
>
> Very respectfully, your obedient servant,
> U. S. Grant

Under a white flag the note began its journey to Lee's hands. That evening Lee read it and silently handed it to General Longstreet. "Not yet," Longstreet said. Lee wrote back:

> Though not entertaining the opinion you express of the hopelessness of further resistance on the part of the Army of Northern Virginia, I reciprocate your desire to avoid useless effusion of blood, and ask the terms you will offer on condition of its surrender.

In his mind there arose the specter of chained captives, traitors taken in shackles to rows of gibbets. Grant sent a reply saying that the only condition he would insist on was that the men who laid down their arms pledge not to take them up again.

While Grant's reply was on its way to Lee, the Confederates kept their westward course, mules falling dead in the mud, famished men eating wild onions, grass, last year's rotted potatoes, anything.

In the morning Henry Wise, formerly governor of Virginia, now a general, found Lee on the rear portico of the house he was using as headquarters. "General Lee," Wise said, "my poor, brave men are lying on yonder hill more dead than alive. For more than a week they have been fighting day and night without food, and, by God, sir, they shall not move another step until somebody gives them something to eat."

"Come in, General," Lee said soothingly. "They deserve something to eat and shall have it, and you shall share my breakfast."

Lee then asked Wise's opinion of the situation they faced. "Situation!" Wise exploded. "There is no situation! Nothing remains, General Lee, but to put your poor men on your poor mules and send them home in time for spring plowing. This army is hopelessly whipped."

"Oh, General, do not talk so wildly. What would the country think of me if I did what you suggest?"

"Country be damned! There is no country. There has been no country, General, for a year or more. You are the country to these men. They have fought for you. They have shivered through a long winter for you. If you demand the sacrifice, there are still thousands of us who will die for you. That is why I say to you, sir, that the blood of any man killed hereafter is upon your head."

Lee said nothing but stood for some time at an open window, studying the crowd of men fleeing west through the fields.

Later that day the Reverend William N. Pendleton, serving as chief of artillery for the Army of Northern Virginia, went to Lee and said that he and several other high officers had agreed that the situation was hopeless. They made their opinions known to their commander, Pendleton said, in order to relieve him of having to take the full responsibility for an offer to surrender.

"I trust it has not come to that!" Lee said. Sooner than accede to a demand by General Grant for unconditional surrender, Lee said, he would die at his post.

Grant's letter saying he asked only that men lay down their arms was delivered. Lee read it and wrote back that in his previous note, "I did not intend to propose surrender but to ask the terms of your proposition." General Lee wrote he would be glad to meet Grant for a discussion of how peace could be restored, and he asked for a meeting at ten the next morning.

His note reached Grant just after midnight on April 9. A courier brought it to the house he was staying in and woke up the staff by calling, "Dispatches for General Grant!" The note went upstairs to Grant, who discussed it with Rawlins. "He did not propose to surrender!" Rawlins said angrily. "That's cool, but a falsehood. He *did* propose, in his heart, to surrender. Now he wants to arrange for peace, something beyond and above the surrender of his army. No, sir. He has to surrender, and nothing else!"

Grant's voice was soft and persuasive. "Some allowance must be made for the trying position in which General Lee is placed. He is compelled to defer somewhat to the wishes of his government. But it all means precisely the same thing. If I meet Lee, he will surrender before I leave."

Grant wrote:

As I have no authority to treat on the subject of peace, the meeting proposed for 10 a.m. today could lead to no good. I will state, however, General, that I am equally anxious for peace with yourself, and the whole North entertains the same feeling. By the South laying down their arms they will hasten that most desirable event.

At that moment John Gordon's men were moving to attack the Yankee cavalry that was blocking the last direction of retreat. "I will strike that man a blow in the morning," Lee had said the previous evening. If Gordon's infantry now encountered only cavalry, the enemy could be pushed aside. If there was infantry behind the cavalry, the problem would be quite different.

Off to the east, the Union infantry rushed through the darkness toward where their cavalry was struggling against Gordon's push. Sometime around nine in the morning they heard heavy firing up ahead. They were put into double-time march, and panting and sweating, they went through woods and out into a field and up a ridge, where their cavalry was falling back. They heard the Confederate artillery fire. A shell crashed into a barn on the ridge, and the building burst into flames. As the Federal cavalry retired, the infantry went forward. Three quarters of a mile away was another ridge, at the foot of which was the Confederate skirmish line, the rifle pits clearly visible.

The Confederate infantry had not opened up, but their artillery was firing. The Union men waited for the Confederates to start shooting, but nothing happened. Then they saw a white flag advancing.

"Tell General Lee," General Gordon said, "I have fought my corps to a frazzle, and I fear I can do nothing unless I am heavily supported by

Longstreet's corps." But Longstreet was holding off thousands of Federals in the rear. The Army of Northern Virginia was caught, surrounded.

Lee heard Gordon's message without a word. Then he spoke as to himself. "There is nothing left me to do but to go and see General Grant, and I would rather die a thousand deaths."

He ordered a flag of truce.

Earlier, away to the west, Grant and Rawlins had set out to join Sheridan at the head of the Union advance. At eleven o'clock they stopped to rest by some burning logs, from which they lighted their cigars. They heard a man shouting and turned to see one of Meade's staff officers on a coal-black stallion that was white with foam. The officer was waving his hat. He jumped off his mount, saluted and handed over a sealed envelope. Rawlins took the envelope and handed it to Grant. Nobody said anything. Grant read the message mechanically, handed it back to Rawlins and said in his usual voice, "You had better read it aloud."

Rawlins took a deep breath and read, "I received your note of this morning with reference to the surrender of this army. I now request an interview for that purpose."

There was silence for a moment. No one looked at anyone else. Then an artillery officer jumped on a log, waved his hat and proposed three cheers. A feeble hurrah came from a few throats and ended brokenly as men began to cry.

Lee lay resting on fence rails covered with blankets, under an apple tree. He was wearing a new uniform with embroidered belt, new gauntlets, high boots with red silk stitchings on their tops and gold spurs at the heels, a sash and a gilded presentation sword whose hilt was formed in the head of a lion. "I have probably to be Grant's prisoner, and I thought I must make my best appearance," he said to one of his generals. The firing had died, and all along the heights appeared noiseless dark blue columns, a great host that looked below on white flags.

A little after midday a Confederate staff officer and a Union colonel came riding up to Lee. "General Lee," said the Confederate officer, "allow me to introduce you to Colonel Babcock."

Grant's aide Orville E. Babcock saluted. Lee stood up. Never had he looked grander. He bowed. Babcock handed over a letter. Under the apple tree, Lee read Grant's acceptance of his offer to meet to arrange the surrender.

He ordered Traveller saddled and asked an aide, Charles Marshall, to go with him on his last mission. They set out with Babcock and a Confederate sergeant, George Tucker, who waved a white handkerchief as they road along—a sign that the truce was in effect. Through silent lines of men they went. Word flew to Grant that they would meet in the little hamlet of Appomattox Court House: two dozen houses, two dirt streets. It was Palm Sunday afternoon, April 9, 1865. Four years less three days had elapsed since the first shell screamed down on Fort Sumter.

As Lee passed, some of his troops broke into cheers. He waved his hand to silence them, in fear that any excitement might bring a shattering of the truce.

The riders came to the outskirts of the hamlet. They halted and waited there while Marshall and Tucker went to find a suitable place where the two commanders could meet.

The first townsman Marshall saw was Wilmer McLean, who offered the use of his house, a substantial dwelling with a well-furnished front parlor. Marshall sent Tucker back to tell Lee. With Babcock at his side, Lee rode to the house, dismounted and went up the stairs. Outside, the street filled up with Union officers.

Half an hour later came Ulysses S. Grant, riding with one hand in his pocket. He had ridden more than thirty-five miles that day over Virginia's muddy springtime roads. He wore the uniform of a private, with lieutenant general's stars sewn on.

Grant got off Cincinnati, who went to munching the spring grass by Traveller's side, and mounted the steps of the McLean house, alone, dirty, no sword, no sash. Mexico came into his mind, he told people later, Mexico and a colonel telling him that General Scott wanted officers to come to headquarters in full uniform. Embarrassment and a strange depression seized him—embarrassment that Lee might now think he had come covered with mud and in a private's crude clothing to rub salt into a wound, depression because of the mission he was on, to demand surrender of a man who had fought so long and hard, so nobly.

"General Lee."

"General Grant."

"I met you once before, General Lee, while we were serving in Mexico.

I have always remembered your appearance, and I think I should have recognized you anywhere."

Seated at small tables ten feet apart, Lee and Grant began talking about Mexico and then the weather in Virginia. Finally Grant signaled Marshall and Babcock to invite in the other gentlemen. Some one dozen Union officers quietly filed in. Then Lee said, "I suppose, General Grant, that the object of our present meeting is fully understood. I asked to see you to ascertain upon what terms you would receive the surrender of my army."

It must have been a relief for Grant to have Lee bring up the subject. Grant had been reluctant, his officers saw, to mention it himself. "The terms I propose," he said, "are those stated substantially in my letter of yesterday—officers and men to be paroled and disqualified from taking up arms again, and all arms, ammunition and supplies to be delivered up as captured property."

"Those are about the conditions I expected would be proposed," Lee said. There would be no triumphal march with prisoners in tow, no hangings.

"Very well, I will write them out." Grant took an order book and started writing in pencil. In the midst of his work he paused and looked at Lee's elegant saber hanging from a gold-braid sword belt. When he was finished, he rose and handed Lee the draft. It struck the watching Federal officers how deliberate Lee's actions were as he placed the order book on the table in front of him, pushed away two candleholders, put a pair of glasses on his nose, crossed his legs and began to read. The room was entirely silent. He came to Grant's final sentences: "The arms, artillery, and private property to be turned over to the officer appointed by me to receive them. This will not embrace the side arms of the officers. This done, each officer and man will be allowed to return to their homes, not to be disturbed by United States authority so long as they observe their paroles."

He looked up at Grant. "This will have a very happy effect on my army," he said. The elegant sword would not have to be handed over in days-of-chivalry display. "There is one thing I would like to mention," Lee said. "The cavalrymen and artillerist own their own horses in our army. I would like to understand whether these men will be permitted to retain their horses."

Grant responded. "I take it that most men in the ranks are small farmers, and as the country has been so raided by the two armies, it is doubtful they will be able to put in a crop to carry themselves and their families through the next winter without the aid of the horses they are now riding, and I will arrange it this way."

"This will have the best possible effect upon the men," Lee said. "It will do much toward conciliating our people."

The letter was given to an officer for copying. Grant signed the copy, and Lee told Marshall how to reply. Marshall wrote:

> Lieut-Gen. U. S. Grant:
> I have received your letter of this date containing the terms of surrender of the Army of Northern Virginia as proposed by you. As they are substantially the same as those expressed in your letter of the 8th instant, they are accepted.
>
> Very respectfully, your obedient servant

Lee signed, and the letters were exchanged. It was over.

By now it was getting on toward four o'clock. After saying a few polite words to one another, the two generals stood up and shook hands. Lee bowed to other men, then went through the door, carrying his hat and gloves. Some Federal officers sitting on the porch sprang up and saluted. He mechanically returned the honor. He gazed out over the yard, past the village, to the little valley where his army was. He drew on his gloves slowly and then absently banged his fists together several times. Traveller and Sergeant Tucker were out of sight. He roused himself and called, "Orderly! Orderly!"

"Here, General, here!" Tucker cried from around the corner. He brought the horse and Lee mounted. A long sigh came from him—"almost a groan," one officer later wrote. Marshall came down the steps and got on his horse. Behind him came Ulysses Grant and the other Union officers.

Grant stopped and took off his hat. His men followed his example. Lee looked at them, raised his hat in silence, turned Traveller and rode back to what had been his army.

As he approached the Confederate lines, a cheer from the troops along the road greeted him, but it died off very suddenly when they saw Lee's face. The road was crowded with men. More men came running, hats off, to pack themselves about him as he slowly made his way. He tried to go on, but the press of bodies halted the horse.

"General, are we surrendered?" a man asked.

Lee took off his hat. "Men," he said, "we have fought the war together, and I have done the best I could for you." His voice was ragged. "You will all be paroled and go to your homes." Tears came into his eyes. His lips moved and formed a soundless, broken attempt at "good-bye."

He pressed Traveller through them. "Good-bye, General, God bless you," he heard over and over from men weeping and touching the horse and his boots. Hat in hand, tears running down his face, Lee said farewell again and again and in broken phrases told his veterans to go home, plant a crop and obey the law. Victorious generals are always cheered by their men, but history knew no such precedent for a commander defeated.

Grant rode away to where his camp would be that night. Hearing the sound of gun salutes from his lines, he ordered the firing stopped. "The Confederates are our countrymen again," he said. He got to the camp and sat in front of his tent, despite a slight shower coming down. Bands played. "Ingalls," he said to an aide, "do you remember that old white mule—" and he talked about someone's mount back in Mexico.

In the morning, by prearrangement, they met again. Surrounded by Yankee officers, they sat their horses just outside the village. They talked for nearly an hour in a drizzling rain, Grant suggesting that Lee meet with Lincoln. "Whatever you and he agree on will be satisfactory to the reasonable people of the North and South."

"General Grant, you know that I am a soldier of the Confederate Army, and I cannot meet Mr. Lincoln. I do not know what Mr. Davis is going to do, and I cannot undertake to make any terms." They saluted each other, and Grant rode back to his tent to pack for City Point. Lee prepared a last message to his men:

After four years of arduous service marked by unsurpassed courage and fortitude, the Army of Northern Virginia has been compelled to yield to overwhelming numbers and resources.

I need not tell the brave survivors of so many hard fought battles, who have remained steadfast to the last, that I have consented to this result from no distrust of them; but feeling that valor and devotion could accomplish nothing that could compensate for the loss that must have attended the continuance of the contest, I determined to avoid useless sacrifice.

With an unceasing admiration of your constancy and devotion to your Country, and a grateful remembrance of your generous consideration for myself, I bid you all an affectionate farewell.

Grant went to City Point. He had telegraphed Julia he would arrive in time for dinner. She had it prepared in the galley of the dispatch boat and then, dressed to the nines, sat with the wives of two other generals and waited. A telegram arrived saying the general was delayed. At four in the morning Julia lay down in her berth, fully dressed, to awaken in broad daylight with her husband standing over her. The dinner was eaten as breakfast. When it was over, Julia asked if he would be going to Richmond.

"I would not distress these people," Grant said. "They are feeling their defeat bitterly, and you would not add to it by my witnessing their despair, would you?"

Instead they went to Washington. The city was wildly celebrating. Buildings were illuminated, bands were playing, and across the Potomac, a thousand freed slaves gathered on the grounds of what had been Robert E.

Lee's estate and was now the property of the United States of America. The freedmen sang "The Year of Jubilee" as rockets shot into the air. Signs in the city read U.S. Army Navy, U.S. Grant.

Grant sat in at a Cabinet meeting, and the President asked if anything had been heard from Sherman in North Carolina, where it was expected that, following Lee's example, Joe Johnson would shortly surrender his forces. Grant replied he was hourly expecting news, and Lincoln said he had reason to believe it likely. There was a dream he had had several times, he explained; it preceded every great event of the war—Fort Sumter, Bull Run, Antietam, Gettysburg, Vicksburg and other battles. He seemed in his dream to be "in some singular, indescribable vessel" that was moving rapidly "towards an indefinite shore." "I had this strange dream again last night," Lincoln said, "and we shall, judging from the past, have great news shortly."

After the meeting, the President asked Grant if the general and his wife would join him and the First Lady in a visit to the theater that night. Grant tentatively accepted, but Julia Grant told her husband she would not spend an evening in the company of the woman whose behavior had been so upsetting back at City Point when she had insulted Mrs. Ord. The President would have to be told that the Grants were going off to visit their children, who were in school in New Jersey. Grant complied with her wish. Ever after he wondered what would have happened had he been in Ford's Theatre that evening.

General Lee stayed in Appomattox until the last parole was made out for the last Confederate, and the last flag surrendered and the last musket stacked for the conqueror to take home.

It was over. Six hundred and twenty thousand men were dead, more than a quarter million southern, more than three hundred and fifty thousand northern. Robert E. Lee, on Traveller, set off on the road to Richmond, followed by his old headquarters wagon and an ambulance carrying an ill member of his staff. He declined to stay in private homes along the way, but pitched his tent as he had during the war.

News of his journey ran ahead of him. When he got to Richmond, a throng was waiting along the route he would have to take into the city. The people were silent, with hats off, wrote one witness. "There was no excitement, no hurrahing; but as the great chief passed, a deep, loving murmur arose from the very hearts of the crowd. Taking off his hat and simply bowing his head, the great man passed silently to his own door; it closed upon him and his people had seen him for the last time in his battle harness."

In June, two months after the surrender, Grant went to West Point, which he had not seen since leaving it, to attend the graduation ceremonies and to go to the nearby residence of Winfield Scott and receive greetings "from the oldest general to the greatest general." Then he returned to Galena, where thousands of people came out to see him pass under triumphal arches and where a huge sign referred to what he had once said he would do if he were mayor of the town: *General, the sidewalk is built.* A committee of citizens presented him with another house. He went to his parents' place near Cincinnati, and Hannah Grant in her apron said, "Well, Ulysses, you've become a great man, haven't you?" and went back to her household tasks.

⚜

Acknowledgments

THE EDITOR AND PUBLISHERS gratefully acknowledge permission to use copyrighted material in this volume. While every effort has been made to secure permissions, if we have failed to acknowledge copyrighted material, we apologize and will make suitable acknowledgment in any future edition.

American Youth Foundation and Ralston-Purina Company for "You Can Be Bigger Than You Are" from *I Dare You*, by William H. Danforth.

McGraw-Hill, Inc., for "Lee and Grant at Appomattox" from *A Dual Biography: Lee and Grant*, by Gene Smith, copyright 1984.

The Helen Steiner Rice Foundation for "Look on the Sunny Side," by Helen Steiner Rice, used with permission of the Helen Steiner Rice Foundation, Cincinnati, Ohio.

young people of Philadelphia were before me now and I could say just this one thing, and that they would remember it. I would give a lifetime for the effect it would have on our city and on civilization. Abraham Lincoln's principle for greatness can be adopted by nearly all. This was his rule: Whatsoever he had to do at all, he put his whole mind into it and held it all there until that was all done. That makes men great almost anywhere. He stuck to those papers at that table and did not look up at me, and I sat there trembling.

Finally, when he had put the string around his papers, he pushed them over to one side and looked over to me, and a smile came over his worn face. He said: "I am a very busy man and have only a few minutes to spare. Now tell me in the fewest words what it is you want." I began to tell him, and mentioned the case, and he said: "I have heard all about it and you do not need to say any more. Mr. Stanton, the Secretary of War, was talking to me only a few days ago about that. You can go to the hotel and rest assured that the President never did sign an order to shoot a boy under twenty years of age, and never will. You can say that to his mother anyhow."

Then he said to me, "How is it going in the field?" I said, "We sometimes get discouraged." And he said: "It is all right. We are going to win out now. We are getting very near the light. No man ought to wish to be President of the United States, and I will be glad when I get through; then Tad and I are going out to Springfield, Illinois. I have bought a farm out there and I don't care if I again earn only twenty-five cents a day. Tad has a mule team, and we are going to plant onions."

Then he asked me, "Were you brought up on a farm?" I said, "Yes; in the

121

Berkshire Hills of Massachusetts." He then threw his leg over the corner of the big chair and said, "I have heard many a time, every since I was young, that up there in those hills you have to sharpen the noses of the sheep in order to get down to the grass between the rocks." He was so familiar, so everyday, so farmer-like, that I felt right at home with him at once.

He then took hold of another roll of paper, and looked up at me and said, "Good morning." I took the hint then and got up and went out. After I had gotten out I could not realize I had seen the President of the United States. But a few days later, when still in the city, I saw the crowd pass through the East Room by the coffin of Abraham Lincoln, and when I looked at the upturned face of the murdered President I felt then that the man I had seen such a short time before, who, so simple a man, so plain a man, was one of the greatest men that God ever raised up to lead a nation on to ultimate liberty. Yet he was only "Old Abe" to his neighbors. When they had the second funeral, I was invited among others, and went out to see that same coffin put back in the tomb at Springfield. Around the tomb stood Lincoln's old neighbors, to whom he was just "Old Abe." Of course that is all they would say.

Did you ever see a man who struts around altogether too large to notice an ordinary working mechanic? Do you think he is great? He is nothing but a puffed-up balloon, held down by his big feet. There is no greatness there.

Who are the great men and women? My attention was called the other day to the history of a very little thing that made the fortune of a very poor man. It was an awful thing, and yet because of that experience he—not a